Presented to: _____

By: _____

God's Promises®
for Men

THOMAS NELSON
Since 1798

NASHVILLE   DALLAS   MEXICO CITY   RIO DE JANEIRO   BEIJING

ISBN: 0-8499-5619-6
ISBN: 0-8499-5621-8 (S.E.)

Printed in the United States of America

Contents

God Challenges a Man to . . .

God Listens to a Man's Prayer When . . .

God Fills a Man with Joy When . . .

God Keeps a Man Secure When . . .

God Comforts a Man When . . .

God's Love Is with a Man When . . .

God Rejoices When a Man . . .

Dynamic Examples of Godly Men

God's Plan for Men Is . . .

To Worship God

And you shall remember the LORD your God, for it is He who gives you power to get wealth, that He may establish His covenant which He swore to your fathers, as it is this day. Then it shall be, if you by any means forget the LORD your God, and follow other gods, and serve them and worship them, I testify against you this day that you shall surely perish.

Deuteronomy 8:18–19

God is Spirit, and those who worship Him must worship in spirit and truth.

John 4:24

For the LORD is the great God,
And the great King above all gods.
In His hand are the deep places of the earth;
The heights of the hills are His also.
The sea is His, for He made it;
And His hands formed the dry land.
Oh come, let us worship and bow down;
Let us kneel before the LORD our Maker.
For He is our God,
And we are the people of His pasture,
And the sheep of His hand.

Psalm 95:3–7

The world is passing away, and the lust of it:
but he who does the will of God abides forever.

1 John 2:17

The LORD is great and greatly to be praised;
He is to be feared above all gods.
Give to the LORD the glory due His name,
Bring an offering, and come into His courts.
Oh, worship the LORD in the beauty of
    holiness!
Tremble before Him, all the earth.

Psalm 96:4, 8–9

Fear God and give glory to Him, for the hour
of His judgment has come; and worship Him who
made heaven and earth, the sea and springs of
water.

Revelation 14:7

Looking unto Jesus, the author and finisher
of our faith, who for the joy that was set before
Him endured the cross, despising the shame, and
has sat down at the right hand of the throne of
God.
    For consider Him who endured such hostil-
ity from sinners against Himself, lest you become
weary and discouraged in your souls.

Hebrews 12:2–3

Now I, John, saw and heard these things. And when I heard and saw, I fell down to worship before the feet of the angel who showed me these things.

Then he said to me, "See that you do not do that. For I am your fellow servant, and of your brethren the prophets, and of those who keep the words of this book. Worship God."

Revelation 22:8–9

Exalt the LORD our God,
And worship at His footstool—
He is holy.

Exalt the LORD our God,
And worship at His holy hill;
For the LORD our God is holy.

Psalm 99:5, 9

Finally, my brethren, rejoice in the Lord.
We are the circumcision, who worship God in the Spirit, rejoice in Christ Jesus, and have no confidence in the flesh.

Philippians 3:1a, 3

To Obey God's Word 🍃

From there you will seek the LORD your God, and you will find Him if you seek Him with all your heart and with all your soul. When you are in distress, and all these things come upon you in the latter days, when you turn to the LORD your God and obey His voice (for the LORD your God is a merciful God), He will not forsake you nor destroy you, nor forget the covenant of your fathers which He swore to them.

Deuteronomy 4:29–31

Jesus answered him, saying, "It is written, 'Man shall not live by bread alone, but by every word of God.'"

Luke 4:4

As for God, His way is perfect;
The word of the LORD is proven;
He is a shield to all who trust in Him.

Psalm 18:30

Oh, that they had such a heart in them that they would fear Me and always keep all My commandments, that it might be well with them and with their children forever!

Deuteronomy 5:29

Whatever things were written before were written for our learning, that we through the patience and comfort of the Scriptures might have hope.

Romans 15:4

The word of God is living and powerful, and sharper than any two-edged sword, piercing even to the division of soul and spirit, and of joints and marrow, and is a discerner of the thoughts and intents of the heart.

Hebrews 4:12

As newborn babes, desire the pure milk of the word, that you may grow thereby.

1 Peter 2:2

The law of the LORD is perfect, converting
    the soul;
The testimony of the LORD is sure, making
    wise the simple;
The statutes of the LORD are right,
    rejoicing the heart;
The commandment of the LORD is pure,
    enlightening the eyes.

Psalm 19:7–8

I understand more than the ancients,
Because I keep Your precepts.
I have restrained my feet from every evil way,
That I may keep Your word.

Psalm 119:100–101

You shall observe My judgments and keep
My ordinances, to walk in them: I am the LORD
your God.

Leviticus 18:4

Draw near to God and He will draw near to
you. Cleanse your hands, you sinners; and purify
your hearts, you double-minded.

James 4:8

As for God, His way is perfect;
The word of the LORD is proven;
He is a shield to all who trust in Him.

Psalm 18:30

To Come to God in Prayer

Ask, and it will be given to you; seek, and you will find; knock, and it will be opened to you. For everyone who asks receives, and he who seeks finds, and to him who knocks it will be opened.

Matthew 7:7–8

Be anxious for nothing, but in everything by prayer and supplication, with thanksgiving, let your requests be made known to God; and the peace of God, which surpasses all understanding, will guard your hearts and minds through Christ Jesus.

Philippians 4:6–7

And whatever things you ask in prayer, believing, you will receive.

Matthew 21:22

Rejoice always, pray without ceasing, in everything give thanks; for this is the will of God in Christ Jesus for you.

1 Thessalonians 5:16–18

If My people who are called by My name will humble themselves, and pray and seek My face, and turn from their wicked ways, then I will hear from heaven, and will forgive their sin and heal their land.

2 Chronicles 7:14

Again I say to you that if two of you agree
on earth concerning anything that they ask, it
will be done for them by My Father in heaven.

Matthew 18:19

Praying always with all prayer and supplication in the Spirit, being watchful to this end
with all perseverance and supplication for all
the saints.

Ephesians 6:18

Hear a just cause, O LORD,
Attend to my cry;
Give ear to my prayer which is not from
    deceitful lips.

Psalm 17:1

For the eyes of the LORD are on the
    righteous,
And His ears are open to their prayers;
But the face of the LORD is against
    those who do evil.

1 Peter 3:12

Hear me when I call, O God of my
    righteousness!
You have relieved me in my distress;
Have mercy on me, and hear my prayer.

Psalm 4:1

To Listen to the Holy Spirit

As His divine power has given to us all things that pertain to life and godliness, through the knowledge of Him who called us by glory and virtue, by which have been given to us exceedingly great and precious promises, that through these you may be partakers of the divine nature, having escaped the corruption that is in the world through lust.

2 Peter 1:3–4

But those who wait on the LORD
Shall renew their strength;
They shall mount up with wings like eagles,
They shall run and not be weary,
They shall walk and not faint.

Isaiah 40:31

But the fruit of the Spirit is love, joy, peace, longsuffering, kindness, goodness, faithfulness, gentleness, self-control. Against such there is no law. And those who are Christ's have crucified the flesh with its passions and desires. If we live in the Spirit, let us also walk in the Spirit.

Galatians 5:22–25

Your ears shall hear a word behind you, saying,
"This is the way, walk in it,"
Whenever you turn to the right hand
Or whenever you turn to the left.

Isaiah 30:21

If you ask anything in My name, I will do it.

If you love Me, keep My commandments. And I will pray the Father, and He will give you another Helper, that He may abide with you forever—the Spirit of truth, whom the world cannot receive, because it neither sees Him nor knows Him; but you know Him, for He dwells with you and will be in you. I will not leave you orphans; I will come to you.

But the Helper, the Holy Spirit, whom the Father will send in My name, He will teach you all things, and bring to your remembrance all things that I said to you.

John 14:14, 15–18, 26

Nevertheless I tell you the truth. It is to your advantage that I go away; for if I do not go away, the Helper will not come to you; but if I depart, I will send Him to you.

However, when He, the Spirit of truth, has come, He will guide you into all truth; for He will not speak on His own authority, but whatever He hears He will speak; and He will tell you things to come.

John 16:7, 13

Being assembled together with them, He commanded them not to depart from Jerusalem, but to wait for the Promise of the Father, "which," He said, "you have heard from Me; for John truly baptized with water, but you shall be baptized with the Holy Spirit not many days from now."

"But you shall receive power when the Holy Spirit has come upon you; and you shall be witnesses to Me in Jerusalem, and in all Judea and Samaria, and to the end of the earth."

Acts 1:4–5, 8

For everyone who asks receives, and he who seeks finds, and to him who knocks it will be opened. If a son asks for bread from any father among you, will he give him a stone? Or if he asks for a fish, will he give him a serpent instead of a fish? Or if he asks for an egg, will he offer him a scorpion? If you then, being evil, know how to give good gifts to your children, how much more will your heavenly Father give the Holy Spirit to those who ask Him!

Luke 11:10–13

For it is God who works in you both to will and to do for His good pleasure.

Philippians 2:13

Eye has not seen, nor ear heard,
Nor have entered into the heart of man
The things which God has prepared for
    those who love Him.

But God has revealed them to us through His Spirit. For the Spirit searches all things, yes, the deep things of God. For what man knows the things of a man except the spirit of the man which is in him? Even so no one knows the things of God except the Spirit of God. Now we have received, not the spirit of the world, but the Spirit who is from God, that we might know the things that have been freely given to us by God. These things we also speak, not in words which man's wisdom teaches but which the Holy Spirit teaches, comparing spiritual things with spiritual. But the natural man does not receive the things of the Spirit of God, for they are foolishness to him; nor can he know them, because they are spiritually discerned.

1 Corinthians 2 :9–14

Who also made us sufficient as ministers of the new covenant, not of the letter but of the Spirit; for the letter kills, but the Spirit gives life.

Now the Lord is the Spirit; and where the Spirit of the Lord is, there is liberty. But we all, with unveiled face, beholding as in a mirror the glory of the Lord, are being transformed into the same image from glory to glory, just as by the Spirit of the Lord.

2 Corinthians 3:6, 17–18

If the Spirit of Him who raised Jesus from the dead dwells in you, He who raised Christ from the dead will also give life to your mortal bodies through His Spirit who dwells in you.

The Spirit Himself bears witness with our spirit that we are children of God, and if children, then heirs—heirs of God and joint heirs with Christ, if indeed we suffer with Him, that we may also be glorified together.

For I consider that the sufferings of this present time are not worthy to be compared with the glory which shall be revealed in us.

Likewise the Spirit also helps in our weaknesses. For we do not know what we should pray for as we ought, but the Spirit Himself makes intercession for us with groanings which cannot be uttered. Now He who searches the hearts knows what the mind of the Spirit is, because He makes intercession for the saints according to the will of God.

Romans 8:11, 16–18, 26–27

God Freely Gives to Men . . .

Eternal Hope for Life

Sing to the LORD with thanksgiving;
Sing praises on the harp to our God,
Who covers the heavens with clouds,
Who prepares rain for the earth,
Who makes grass to grow on the mountains.
He gives to the beast its food,
And to the young ravens that cry.
He does not delight in the strength of the
     horse;
He takes no pleasure in the legs of a man.
The LORD takes pleasure in those who fear
     Him,
In those who hope in His mercy.
Praise the LORD, O Jerusalem!
Praise your God, O Zion!
For He has strengthened the bars of your gates;
He has blessed your children within you.

Psalm 147:7–13

But let us who are of the day be sober, putting on the breastplate of faith and love, and as a helmet the hope of salvation. For God did not appoint us to wrath, but to obtain salvation through our Lord Jesus Christ, who died for us, that whether we wake or sleep, we should live together with Him.

Therefore comfort each other and edify one another, just as you also are doing.

1 Thessalonians 5:8–11

But God, who is rich in mercy, because of His great love with which He loved us, even when we were dead in trespasses, made us alive together with Christ (by grace you have been saved), and raised us up together, and made us sit together in the heavenly places in Christ Jesus, that in the ages to come He might show the exceeding riches of His grace in His kindness toward us in Christ Jesus.

Ephesians 2:4–7

If then you were raised with Christ, seek those things which are above, where Christ is, sitting at the right hand of God. Set your mind on things above, not on things on the earth.

Colossians 3:1–2

Knowing that a man is not justified by the works of the law but by faith in Jesus Christ, even we have believed in Christ Jesus, that we might be justified by faith in Christ and not by the works of the law; for by the works of the law no flesh shall be justified.

I have been crucified with Christ; it is no longer I who live, but Christ lives in me; and the life which I now live in the flesh I live by faith in the Son of God, who loved me and gave Himself for me.

Galatians 2:16, 20

For as many as are led by the Spirit of God, these are sons of God. For you did not receive the spirit of bondage again to fear, but you received the Spirit of adoption by whom we cry out, "Abba, Father." The Spirit Himself bears witness with our spirit that we are children of God, and if children, then heirs—heirs of God and joint heirs with Christ, if indeed we suffer with Him, that we may also be glorified together.

For I consider that the sufferings of this present time are not worthy to be compared with the glory which shall be revealed in us.

For we were saved in this hope, but hope that is seen is not hope; for why does one still hope for what he sees? But if we hope for what we do not see, we eagerly wait for it with perseverance.

Romans 8:14–18, 24–25

I have fought the good fight, I have finished the race, I have kept the faith. Finally, there is laid up for me the crown of righteousness, which the Lord, the righteous Judge, will give to me on that Day, and not to me only but also to all who have loved His appearing.

2 Timothy 4:7–8

Blessed be the God and Father of our Lord Jesus Christ, who according to His abundant mercy has begotten us again to a living hope through the resurrection of Jesus Christ from the dead, to an inheritance incorruptible and undefiled and that does not fade away, reserved in heaven for you, who are kept by the power of God through faith for salvation ready to be revealed in the last time.

In this you greatly rejoice, though now for a little while, if need be, you have been grieved by various trials, that the genuineness of your faith, being much more precious than gold that perishes, though it is tested by fire, may be found to praise, honor, and glory at the revelation of Jesus Christ, whom having not seen you love. Though now you do not see Him, yet believing, you rejoice with joy inexpressible and full of glory, receiving the end of your faith—the salvation of your souls.

1 Peter 1:3–9

Because of the hope which is laid up for you in heaven, of which you heard before in the word of the truth of the gospel, which has come to you, as it has also in all the world, and is bringing forth fruit, as it is also among you since the day you heard and knew the grace of God in truth.

Colossians 1:5–6

Wisdom for Each Day

My son, pay attention to my wisdom;
Lend your ear to my understanding,
That you may preserve discretion,
And your lips may keep knowledge.

Proverbs 5:1–2

The fear of the LORD is the beginning of
    wisdom;
A good understanding have all those who do
    His commandments.
His praise endures forever.

Psalm 111:10

The days of our lives are seventy years;
And if by reason of strength they are eighty
    years,
Yet their boast is only labor and sorrow;
For it is soon cut off, and we fly away.
Who knows the power of Your anger?
For as the fear of You, so is Your wrath.
So teach us to number our days,
That we may gain a heart of wisdom.

Psalm 90:10–12

How much better to get wisdom than gold!
And to get understanding is to be chosen
    rather than silver.

Proverbs 16:16

Get wisdom! Get understanding!
Do not forget, nor turn away from the words
    of my mouth.
Do not forsake her, and she will preserve
    you;
Love her, and she will keep you.
Wisdom is the principal thing;
Therefore get wisdom.
And in all your getting, get understanding.
Exalt her, and she will promote you;
She will bring you honor, when you embrace
    her.
She will place on your head an ornament of
    grace;
A crown of glory she will deliver to you.
Hear, my son, and receive my sayings,
And the years of your life will be many.
I have taught you in the way of wisdom;
I have led you in right paths.

Proverbs 4:5–11

However, we speak wisdom among those
who are mature, yet not the wisdom of this age,
nor of the rulers of this age, who are coming to
nothing. But we speak the wisdom of God in a
mystery, the hidden wisdom which God ordained
before the ages for our glory, which none of the
rulers of this age knew; for had they known, they
would not have crucified the Lord of glory.

1 Corinthians 2:6–8

Happy is the man who finds wisdom,
And the man who gains understanding;
For her proceeds are better than the profits of
    silver,
And her gain than fine gold.
She is more precious than rubies,
And all the things you may desire cannot
    compare with her.
Length of days is in her right hand,
In her left hand riches and honor.
Her ways are ways of pleasantness,
And all her paths are peace.
She is a tree of life to those who take hold of
    her,
And happy are all who retain her.
The LORD by wisdom founded the earth;
By understanding He established the heavens;
By His knowledge the depths were broken up,
And clouds drop down the dew.
My son, let them not depart from your
    eyes—
Keep sound wisdom and discretion;
So they will be life to your soul
And grace to your neck.

Proverbs 3:13–22

But the wisdom that is from above is first pure, then peaceable, gentle, willing to yield, full of mercy and good fruits, without partiality and without hypocrisy.

James 3:17

If any of you lacks wisdom, let him ask of God, who gives to all liberally and without reproach, and it will be given to him. But let him ask in faith, with no doubting, for he who doubts is like a wave of the sea driven and tossed by the wind.

James 1:5–6

The fear of the LORD is the beginning of
    wisdom,
And the knowledge of the Holy One is
    understanding.
If you are wise, you are wise for yourself,
And if you scoff, you will bear it alone.

Proverbs 9:10, 12

A wise man fears and departs from evil,
But a fool rages and is self-confident.

Proverbs 14:16

My son, keep my words,
And treasure my commands within you.
Keep my commands and live,
And my law as the apple of your eye.
Bind them on your fingers;
Write them on the tablet of your heart.
Say to wisdom, "You are my sister,"
And call understanding your nearest kin,
That they may keep you from the immoral
    woman,
From the seductress who flatters with her
    words.

Proverbs 7:1–5

Victory Over Sin

Therefore, if anyone is in Christ, he is a new creation; old things have passed away; behold, all things have become new. Now all things are of God, who has reconciled us to Himself through Jesus Christ, and has given us the ministry of reconciliation, that is, that God was in Christ reconciling the world to Himself, not imputing their trespasses to them, and has committed to us the word of reconciliation.

Now then, we are ambassadors for Christ, as though God were pleading through us: we implore you on Christ's behalf, be reconciled to God. For He made Him who knew no sin to be sin for us, that we might become the righteousness of God in Him.

2 Corinthians 5:17–21

O God, You know my foolishness;
And my sins are not hidden from You.
Psalm 69:5

For as many as are of the works of the law are under the curse; for it is written, "Cursed is everyone who does not continue in all things which are written in the book of the law, to do them." But that no one is justified by the law in the sight of God is evident, for "the just shall live by faith."
Galatians 3:10–11

Stand fast therefore in the liberty by which Christ has made us free, and do not be entangled again with a yoke of bondage.

Galatians 5:1

"Wash yourselves, make yourselves clean;
Put away the evil of your doings from
     before My eyes.
Cease to do evil,
Learn to do good;
Seek justice,
Rebuke the oppressor;
Defend the fatherless,
Plead for the widow."
"Come now, and let us reason together,"
     Says the LORD,
"Though your sins are like scarlet,
They shall be as white as snow;
Though they are red like crimson,
They shall be as wool.
If you are willing and obedient,
You shall eat the good of the land."

Isaiah 1:16–19

Therefore, since we have this ministry, as we have received mercy, we do not lose heart. But we have renounced the hidden things of shame, not walking in craftiness nor handling the word of God deceitfully, but by manifestation of the truth commending ourselves to every man's conscience in the sight of God. But even if our gospel is veiled, it is veiled to those who are perishing, whose minds the god of this age has blinded, who do not believe, lest the light of the gospel of the glory of Christ, who is the image of God, should shine on them. For we do not preach ourselves, but Christ Jesus the Lord, and ourselves your bondservants for Jesus' sake. For it is the God who commanded light to shine out of darkness, who has shone in our hearts to give the light of the knowledge of the glory of God in the face of Jesus Christ.

2 Corinthians 4:1–6

And you know that He was manifested to take away our sins, and in Him there is no sin. Whoever abides in Him does not sin. Whoever sins has neither seen Him nor known Him.

Little children, let no one deceive you. He who practices righteousness is righteous, just as He is righteous.

1 John 3:5–7

Finally, my brethren, be strong in the Lord and in the power of His might. Put on the whole armor of God, that you may be able to stand against the wiles of the devil. For we do not wrestle against flesh and blood, but against principalities, against powers, against the rulers of the darkness of this age, against spiritual hosts of wickedness in the heavenly places. Therefore take up the whole armor of God, that you may be able to withstand in the evil day, and having done all, to stand.

Stand therefore, having girded your waist with truth, having put on the breastplate of righteousness, and having shod your feet with the preparation of the gospel of peace; above all, taking the shield of faith with which you will be able to quench all the fiery darts of the wicked one. And take the helmet of salvation, and the sword of the Spirit, which is the word of God; praying always with all prayer and supplication in the Spirit, being watchful to this end with all perseverance and supplication for all the saints.

Ephesians 6:10–18

This is the message which we have heard from Him and declare to you, that God is light and in Him is no darkness at all. If we say that we have fellowship with Him, and walk in darkness, we lie and do not practice the truth. But if we walk in the light as He is in the light, we have fellowship with one another, and the blood of Jesus Christ His Son cleanses us from all sin.

If we say that we have no sin, we deceive ourselves, and the truth is not in us. If we confess our sins, He is faithful and just to forgive us our sins and to cleanse us from all unrighteousness. If we say that we have not sinned, we make Him a liar, and His word is not in us.

1 John 1:5–10

O Death, where is your sting?
O Hades, where is your victory?
The sting of death is sin, and the strength of sin is the law. But thanks be to God, who gives us the victory through our Lord Jesus Christ.

Therefore, my beloved brethren, be steadfast, immovable, always abounding in the work of the Lord, knowing that your labor is not in vain in the Lord.

1 Corinthians 15:55–58

Peace in Troubled Times

For none of us lives to himself, and no one dies
to himself.

Romans 14:7

A horse is a vain hope for safety;
Neither shall it deliver any by its great strength.
Behold, the eye of the LORD is on those who
    fear Him,
On those who hope in His mercy,
To deliver their soul from death,
And to keep them alive in famine.
Our soul waits for the LORD;
He is our help and our shield.
For our heart shall rejoice in Him,
Because we have trusted in His holy name.
Let Your mercy, O LORD, be upon us,
Just as we hope in You.

Psalm 33:17–22

Turn Yourself to me, and have mercy on
    me,
For I am desolate and afflicted.
The troubles of my heart have enlarged;
Bring me out of my distresses!
Look on my affliction and my pain,
And forgive all my sins.

Psalm 25:16–18

The LORD builds up Jerusalem;
He gathers together the outcasts of Israel.
He heals the brokenhearted
And binds up their wounds.
Great is our LORD, and mighty in power;
His understanding is infinite.
The LORD lifts up the humble;
He casts the wicked down to the ground.
For He has strengthened the bars of your gates;
He has blessed your children within you.
He makes peace in your borders,
And fills you with the finest wheat.

Psalm 147:2–3, 5–6, 13–14

Peace I leave with you, My peace I give to you; not as the world gives do I give to you. Let not your heart be troubled, neither let it be afraid.

John 14:27

Casting all your care upon Him, for He cares for you.

Be sober, be vigilant; because your adversary the devil walks about like a roaring lion, seeking whom he may devour. Resist him, steadfast in the faith, knowing that the same sufferings are experienced by your brotherhood in the world. But may the God of all grace, who called us to His eternal glory by Christ Jesus, after you have suffered a while, perfect, establish, strengthen, and settle you. To Him be the glory and the dominion forever and ever. Amen.

1 Peter 5:7–11

I will be glad and rejoice in Your mercy,
For You have considered my trouble;
You have known my soul in adversities.

Psalm 31:7

Trust in the LORD with all your heart,
And lean not on your own understanding;
In all your ways acknowledge Him,
And He shall direct your paths.

Proverbs 3:5–6

I will bless the LORD at all times;
His praise shall continually be in my mouth.
My soul shall make its boast in the LORD;
The humble shall hear of it and be glad.
Oh, magnify the LORD with me,
And let us exalt His name together.
I sought the LORD, and He heard me,
And delivered me from all my fears.
They looked to Him and were radiant,
And their faces were not ashamed.
This poor man cried out, and the LORD
          heard him,
And saved him out of all his troubles.
The angel of the LORD encamps all around
          those who fear Him,
And delivers them.
Oh, taste and see that the LORD is good;
Blessed is the man who trusts in Him!

Psalm 34:1–8

Power to Defeat Their Deepest Fears 🌿

Then Jesus spoke to them again, saying, "I am the light of the world. He who follows Me shall not walk in darkness, but have the light of life."

John 8:12

I will love You, O LORD, my strength.
The LORD is my rock and my fortress and
    my deliverer;
My God, my strength, in whom I will trust;
My shield and the horn of my salvation, my
    stronghold.
I will call upon the LORD, who is worthy to
    be praised;
So shall I be saved from my enemies.

Psalm 18:1–3

For You will light my lamp;
The LORD my God will enlighten my
    darkness.
For by You I can run against a troop,
By my God I can leap over a wall.
As for God, His way is perfect;
The word of the LORD is proven;
He is a shield to all who trust in Him.

Psalm 18:28–30

The LORD is my light and my salvation;
Whom shall I fear?
The LORD is the strength of my life;
Of whom shall I be afraid?
When the wicked came against me
To eat up my flesh,
My enemies and foes,
They stumbled and fell.
Though an army may encamp against me,
My heart shall not fear;
Though war may rise against me,
In this I will be confident.
One thing I have desired of the LORD,
That will I seek:
That I may dwell in the house of the LORD
All the days of my life,
To behold the beauty of the LORD,
And to inquire in His temple.
For in the time of trouble
He shall hide me in His pavilion;
In the secret place of His tabernacle
He shall hide me;
He shall set me high upon a rock.

Psalm 27:1–5

Delight yourself also in the LORD,
And He shall give you the desires of your
  heart.
Commit your way to the LORD,
Trust also in Him,
And He shall bring it to pass.
He shall bring forth your righteousness as
  the light,
And your justice as the noonday.

Psalm 37:4–6

Yet in all these things we are more than conquerors through Him who loved us. For I am persuaded that neither death nor life, nor angels nor principalities nor powers, nor things present nor things to come, nor height nor depth, nor any other created thing, shall be able to separate us from the love of God which is in Christ Jesus our Lord.

Romans 8:37–39

Do not be afraid of sudden terror,
Nor of trouble from the wicked when it
  comes;
For the LORD will be your confidence,
And will keep your foot from being caught.

Proverbs 3:25–26

The sun shall no longer be your light by day,
Nor for brightness shall the moon give light
    to you;
But the LORD will be to you an everlasting
    light,
And your God your glory.
Your sun shall no longer go down,
Nor shall your moon withdraw itself;
For the LORD will be your everlasting light,
And the days of your mourning shall be
    ended.

Isaiah 60:19–20

Courage to Be Men of Integrity

Blessed is the man
Who walks not in the counsel of the
      ungodly,
Nor stands in the path of sinners,
Nor sits in the seat of the scornful;
But his delight is in the law of the LORD,
And in His law he meditates day and night.
He shall be like a tree
Planted by the rivers of water,
That brings forth its fruit in its season,
Whose leaf also shall not wither;
And whatever he does shall prosper.
The ungodly are not so,
But are like the chaff which the wind drives
      away.
Therefore the ungodly shall not stand in
      the judgment,
Nor sinners in the congregation of the
      righteous.
For the LORD knows the way of the
      righteous,
But the way of the ungodly shall perish.

Psalm 1:1–6

A good man deals graciously and lends;
He will guide his affairs with discretion.
Surely he will never be shaken;
The righteous will be in everlasting
      remembrance.
He will not be afraid of evil tidings;
His heart is steadfast, trusting in the LORD.

Psalm 112:5–7

Blessed are the undefiled in the way,
Who walk in the law of the LORD!
Blessed are those who keep His testimonies,
Who seek Him with the whole heart!
They also do no iniquity;
They walk in His ways.
You have commanded us
To keep Your precepts diligently.
Oh, that my ways were directed
To keep Your statutes!
Then I would not be ashamed,
When I look into all Your commandments.
I will praise You with uprightness of heart,
When I learn Your righteous judgments.
I will keep Your statutes;
Oh, do not forsake me utterly!

Psalm 119:1–8

Dishonest scales are an abomination to the
    LORD,
But a just weight is His delight.
When pride comes, then comes shame;
But with the humble is wisdom.
The integrity of the upright will guide them,
But the perversity of the unfaithful will
    destroy them.

Proverbs 11:1–3

He who speaks truth declares righteousness,
But a false witness, deceit.
There is one who speaks like the piercings
    of a sword,
But the tongue of the wise promotes health.
The truthful lip shall be established forever,
But a lying tongue is but for a moment.

Proverbs 12:17–19

The righteous man walks in his integrity;
His children are blessed after him.

Proverbs 20:7

The LORD shall judge the peoples;
Judge me, O LORD, according to my
    righteousness,
And according to my integrity within me.

Psalm 7:8

Moreover Job continued his discourse, and said:

"As God lives, who has taken away my justice,
And the Almighty, who has made my soul
 bitter,
As long as my breath is in me,
And the breath of God in my nostrils,
My lips will not speak wickedness,
Nor my tongue utter deceit.
Far be it from me
That I should say you are right;
Till I die I will not put away my integrity
 from me.
My righteousness I hold fast, and will not
 let it go;
My heart shall not reproach me as long as
 I live.

Job 27:1–6

If I have walked with falsehood,
Or if my foot has hastened to deceit,
Let me be weighed on honest scales,
That God may know my integrity.

Job 31:5–6

God Asks a Man to...

Witness to the Lost

Go therefore and make disciples of all the
nations, baptizing them in the name of the Father
and of the Son and of the Holy Spirit, teaching
them to observe all things that I have commanded
you; and lo, I am with you always, even to the end
of the age. Amen.

Matthew 28:19–20

Therefore God also has highly exalted Him
and given Him the name which is above every
name, that at the name of Jesus every knee should
bow, of those in heaven, and of those on earth, and
of those under the earth, and that every tongue
should confess that Jesus Christ is Lord, to the
glory of God the Father.

Philippians 2:9–11

Also I say to you, whoever confesses Me
before men, him the Son of Man also will confess
before the angels of God. But he who denies Me
before men will be denied before the angels of
God.

Luke 12:8–9

I say to you that likewise there will be more joy in heaven over one sinner who repents than over ninety-nine just persons who need no repentance.

Luke 15:7

For the Son of Man has come to seek and to save that which was lost.

Luke 19:10

The Spirit of the LORD is upon Me,
Because He has anointed Me
To preach the gospel to the poor;
He has sent Me to heal the brokenhearted,
To proclaim liberty to the captives
And recovery of sight to the blind,
To set at liberty those who are oppressed.

Luke 4:18

Therefore whoever confesses Me before men, him I will also confess before My Father who is in heaven. But whoever denies Me before men, him I will also deny before My Father who is in heaven.

Matthew 10:32–33

Behold, I stand at the door and knock. If anyone hears My voice and opens the door, I will come in to him and dine with him, and he with Me.

Revelation 3:20

He who has the Son has life; he who does not have the Son of God does not have life.

1 John 5:12

Let your light so shine before men, that they may see your good works and glorify your Father in heaven.

Matthew 5:16

And He said to them, "Go into all the world and preach the gospel to every creature. He who believes and is baptized will be saved; but he who does not believe will be condemned."

Mark 16:15–16

If anyone serves Me, let him follow Me; and where I am, there My servant will be also. If anyone serves Me, him My Father will honor.

John 12:26

For God so loved the world that He gave His only begotten Son, that whoever believes in Him should not perish but have everlasting life. For God did not send His Son into the world to condemn the world, but that the world through Him might be saved.

John 3:16–17

The Lord is not slack concerning His promise, as some count slackness, but is longsuffering toward us, not willing that any should perish but that all should come to repentance.

2 Peter 3:9

Those who are wise shall shine like the brightness of the firmament, and those who turn many to righteousness like the stars forever and ever.

Daniel 12:3

Love His Neighbor

But he, wanting to justify himself, said to Jesus, "And who is my neighbor?"

Then Jesus answered and said: "A certain man went down from Jerusalem to Jericho, and fell among thieves, who stripped him of his clothing, wounded him, and departed, leaving him half dead. Now by chance a certain priest came down that road. And when he saw him, he passed by on the other side. Likewise a Levite, when he arrived at the place, came and looked, and passed by on the other side. But a certain Samaritan, as he journeyed, came where he was. And when he saw him, he had compassion. So he went to him and bandaged his wounds, pouring on oil and wine; and he set him on his own animal, brought him to an inn, and took care of him. On the next day, when he departed, he took out two denarii, gave them to the innkeeper, and said to him, 'Take care of him; and whatever more you spend, when I come again, I will repay you.' So which of these three do you think was neighbor to him who fell among the thieves?"

And he said, "He who showed mercy on him."

Then Jesus said to him, "Go and do likewise."

Luke 10:29–37

You shall love your neighbor as yourself.
Matthew 19:19b

You shall not bear false witness against your neighbor.

You shall not covet your neighbor's house; you shall not covet your neighbor's wife, nor his male servant, nor his female servant, nor his ox, nor his donkey, nor anything that is your neighbor's.
Exodus 20:16–17

He who despises his neighbor sins;
But he who has mercy on the poor,
   happy is he.

Proverbs 14:21

He who is devoid of wisdom despises his
   neighbor,
But a man of understanding holds his peace.
Proverbs 11:12

You shall not cheat your neighbor, nor rob him.

Leviticus 19:13a

Do not go hastily to court;
For what will you do in the end,
When your neighbor has put you to shame?
Debate your case with your neighbor,
And do not disclose the secret to another.
Proverbs 25:8–9

And do not be conformed to this world, but be transformed by the renewing of your mind, that you may prove what is that good and acceptable and perfect will of God.

For I say, through the grace given to me, to everyone who is among you, not to think of himself more highly than he ought to think, but to think soberly, as God has dealt to each one a measure of faith.

Romans 12:2–3

Whoever secretly slanders his neighbor,
Him I will destroy;
The one who has a haughty look and a proud
     heart,
Him I will not endure.
My eyes shall be on the faithful of the land,
That they may dwell with me;
He who walks in a perfect way,
He shall serve me.
He who works deceit shall not dwell within
     my house;
He who tells lies shall not continue in my
     presence.

Psalm 101:5–7

Do not say to your neighbor,
"Go, and come back,
And tomorrow I will give it,"
When you have it with you.
Do not devise evil against your neighbor,
For he dwells by you for safety's sake.

Proverbs 3:28–29

Reach Out to the Poor and Homeless 🍂

Then the King will say to those on His right hand, "Come, you blessed of My Father, inherit the kingdom prepared for you from the foundation of the world: for I was hungry and you gave Me food; I was thirsty and you gave Me drink; I was a stranger and you took Me in; I was naked and you clothed Me; I was sick and you visited Me; I was in prison and you came to Me."

Then the righteous will answer Him, saying, "Lord, when did we see You hungry and feed You, or thirsty and give You drink? When did we see You a stranger and take You in, or naked and clothe You? Or when did we see You sick, or in prison, and come to You?" And the King will answer and say to them, "Assuredly, I say to you, inasmuch as you did it to one of the least of these My brethren, you did it to Me."

Matthew 25:34–40

And above all things have fervent love for one another, for love will cover a multitude of sins. Be hospitable to one another without grumbling. As each one has received a gift, minister it to one another, as good stewards of the manifold grace of God.

1 Peter 4:8–10

Is it not to share your bread with the hungry,
And that you bring to your house the poor
    who are cast out;
When you see the naked, that you cover him,
And not hide yourself from your own flesh?
Then your light shall break forth like the
    morning,
Your healing shall spring forth speedily,
And your righteousness shall go before you;
The glory of the LORD shall be your rear
    guard.
Then you shall call, and the LORD will
    answer;
You shall cry, and He will say, "Here I am."
If you take away the yoke from your midst,
The pointing of the finger, and speaking
    wickedness,
If you extend your soul to the hungry
And satisfy the afflicted soul,
Then your light shall dawn in the darkness,
And your darkness shall be as the noonday.
The LORD will guide you continually,
And satisfy your soul in drought,
And strengthen your bones;
You shall be like a watered garden,
And like a spring of water, whose waters do
    not fail.

Isaiah 58:7–11

Whoever shuts his ears to the cry of the poor
Will also cry himself and not be heard.

Proverbs 21:13

Let brotherly love continue. Do not forget to entertain strangers, for by so doing some have unwittingly entertained angels.

Hebrews 13:1–2

For the needy shall not always be forgotten;
The expectation of the poor shall not perish
     forever.
Arise, O LORD,
Do not let man prevail;
Let the nations be judged in Your sight.

Psalm 9:18–19

When you reap the harvest of your land, you shall not wholly reap the corners of your field, nor shall you gather the gleanings of your harvest. And you shall not glean your vineyard, nor shall you gather every grape of your vineyard; you shall leave them for the poor and the stranger: I am the LORD your God.

Leviticus 19:9–10

Defend the poor and fatherless;
Do justice to the afflicted and needy.
Deliver the poor and needy;
Free them from the hand of the wicked.

Psalm 82:3–4

Happy is he who has the God of Jacob
     for his help,
Whose hope is in the LORD his God,
Who made heaven and earth,
The sea, and all that is in them;
Who keeps truth forever,
Who executes justice for the oppressed,
Who gives food to the hungry.
The LORD gives freedom to the prisoners.
The LORD opens the eyes of the blind;
The LORD raises those who are bowed down;
The LORD loves the righteous.
The LORD watches over the strangers;
He relieves the fatherless and widow;
But the way of the wicked He turns upside
     down.
The LORD shall reign forever—
Your God, O Zion, to all generations.
Praise the LORD!

Psalm 146:5–10

But whoever has this world's goods, and sees
his brother in need, and shuts up his heart from
him, how does the love of God abide in him?

My little children, let us not love in word or
in tongue, but in deed and in truth. And by this
we know that we are of the truth, and shall assure
our hearts before Him.

1 John 3:17–19

If a brother or sister is naked and destitute of daily food, and one of you says to them, "Depart in peace, be warmed and filled," but you do not give them the things which are needed for the body, what does it profit? Thus also faith by itself, if it does not have works, is dead.

James 2:15–17

Trust God

Behold, He who keeps Israel
Shall neither slumber nor sleep.
The LORD is your keeper;
The LORD is your shade at your right
        hand.
The sun shall not strike you by day,
Nor the moon by night.
The LORD shall preserve you from all
        evil;
He shall preserve your soul.
The LORD shall preserve your going out
        and your coming in
From this time forth, and even
        forevermore.

Psalm 121:4–8

Oh, the depth of the riches both of the
wisdom and knowledge of God! How unsearchable are His judgments and His ways past
finding out!

For who has known the mind of the LORD?
Or who has become His counselor?
Or who has first given to Him
And it shall be repaid to him?

For of Him and through Him and to Him
are all things, to whom be glory forever. Amen.

Romans 11:33–36

Then Job answered and said:
"Even today my complaint is bitter;
My hand is listless because of my
groaning."

Job 23:1–2

In the day of my trouble I will call upon You,
For You will answer me.
Among the gods there is none like You, O
    Lord;
Nor are there any works like Your works.
All nations whom You have made
Shall come and worship before You, O Lord,
And shall glorify Your name.
For You are great, and do wondrous things;
You alone are God.

Psalm 86:7–10

Then they cried out to the LORD in their
    trouble,
And He saved them out of their distresses.
He sent His word and healed them,
And delivered them from their destructions.

Psalm 107:19–20

Trust in the LORD with all your heart,
And lean not on your own understanding;
In all your ways acknowledge Him,
And He shall direct your paths.

Proverbs 3:5–6

And he said:
"The LORD is my rock and my fortress and
       my deliverer;
The God of my strength, in whom I will trust;
My shield and the horn of my salvation,
My stronghold and my refuge;
My Savior, You save me from violence."

2 Samuel 22:2–3

Though He slay me, yet will I trust Him.
Even so, I will defend my own ways before
       Him.
He also shall be my salvation.

Job 13:15–16a

But know that the LORD has set apart for
       Himself him who is godly;
The LORD will hear when I call to Him.
Be angry, and do not sin.
Meditate within your heart on your bed,
       and be still.
Offer the sacrifices of righteousness,
And put your trust in the LORD.

Psalm 4:3–5

Preserve me, O God, for in You I put my
       trust.
O my soul, you have said to the LORD,
"You are my Lord,
My goodness is nothing apart from You."

Psalm 16:1–2

Honor and Support His Church and Pastor

And we urge you, brethren, to recognize those who labor among you, and are over you in the Lord and admonish you, and to esteem them very highly in love for their work's sake. Be at peace among yourselves.

1 Thessalonians 5:12–13

Remember those who rule over you, who have spoken the word of God to you, whose faith follow, considering the outcome of their conduct.

Obey those who rule over you, and be submissive, for they watch out for your souls, as those who must give account. Let them do so with joy and not with grief, for that would be unprofitable for you.

Hebrews 13:7, 17

Likewise you younger people, submit yourselves to your elders. Yes, all of you be submissive to one another, and be clothed with humility, for

"God resists the proud,
But gives grace to the humble."

1 Peter 5:5

If we endure,
We shall also reign with Him.
If we deny Him,
He also will deny us.

2 Timothy 2:12

LORD, who may abide in Your tabernacle?
Who may dwell in Your holy hill?
He who walks uprightly,
And works righteousness,
And speaks the truth in his heart.

Psalm 15:1–2

You are complete in Him, who is the head of all principality and power.

And not holding fast to the Head, from whom all the body, nourished and knit together by joints and ligaments, grows with the increase that is from God.

Colossians 2:10–19

For as we have many members in one body, but all the members do not have the same function, so we, being many, are one body in Christ, and individually members of one another.

Romans 12:4–5

Behold, how good and how pleasant it is
For brethren to dwell together in unity!

Psalm 133:1

He Himself gave some to be apostles, some prophets, some evangelists, and some pastors and teachers, for the equipping of the saints for the work of ministry, for the edifying of the body of Christ.

Ephesians 4:11–12

For as the body is one and has many members, but all the members of that one body, being many, are one body, so also is Christ. For by one Spirit we were all baptized into one body— whether Jews or Greeks, whether slaves or free— and have all been made to drink into one Spirit. For in fact the body is not one member but many.

If the foot should say, "Because I am not a hand, I am not of the body," is it therefore not of the body? And if the ear should say, "Because I am not an eye, I am not of the body," is it therefore not of the body? If the whole body were an eye, where would be the hearing? If the whole were hearing, where would be the smelling? But now God has set the members, each one of them, in the body just as He pleased. And if they were all one member, where would the body be?

But now indeed there are many members, yet one body. And the eye cannot say to the hand, "I have no need of you"; nor again the head to the feet, "I have no need of you." No, much rather, those members of the body which seem to be weaker are necessary. And those members of the body which we think to be less honorable, on these we bestow greater honor; and our unpresentable parts have greater modesty, but our presentable parts have no need. But God composed the body, having given greater honor to that part which lacks it, that there should be no schism in the body, but that the members should have the same care for one another. And if one member suffers, all the members suffer with it; or if one member is honored, all the members rejoice with it.

Now you are the body of Christ, and members individually. And God has appointed these in the church: first apostles, second prophets, third teachers, after that miracles, then gifts of healings, helps, administrations, varieties of tongues.

1 Corinthians 12:12–28

God Gives a Man Strength When . . .

He Comforts His Loved Ones

But the mercy of the LORD is from
    everlasting to everlasting
On those who fear Him,
And His righteousness to children's children.
Psalm 103:17

He will feed His flock like a shepherd;
He will gather the lambs with His arm,
And carry them in His bosom,
And gently lead those who are with young.
Isaiah 40:11

Are not two sparrows sold for a copper coin?
And not one of them falls to the ground apart
from your Father's will. But the very hairs of your
head are all numbered. Do not fear therefore; you
are of more value than many sparrows.
Matthew 10:29–31

Now we exhort you, brethren, warn those
who are unruly, comfort the fainthearted, uphold
the weak, be patient with all. See that no one ren-
ders evil for evil to anyone, but always pursue what
is good both for yourselves and for all.
1 Thessalonians 5:14–15

Blessed be the God and Father of our Lord Jesus Christ, the Father of mercies and God of all comfort, who comforts us in all our tribulation, that we may be able to comfort those who are in any trouble, with the comfort with which we ourselves are comforted by God. For as the sufferings of Christ abound in us, so our consolation also abounds through Christ.

2 Corinthians 1:3–5

Fear not, for I am with you;
Be not dismayed, for I am your God.
I will strengthen you,
Yes, I will help you,
I will uphold you with My righteous
    right hand.
Behold, I will make you into a new threshing
    sledge with sharp teeth;
You shall thresh the mountains and beat
    them small,
And make the hills like chaff.
You shall winnow them, the wind shall
    carry them away,
And the whirlwind shall scatter them;
You shall rejoice in the LORD,
And glory in the Holy One of Israel.

Isaiah 41:10, 15–16

When the waves of death surrounded me,
The floods of ungodliness made me afraid.
The sorrows of Sheol surrounded me;
The snares of death confronted me.
In my distress I called upon the LORD,
And cried out to my God;
He heard my voice from His temple,
And my cry entered His ears.

2 Samuel 22:5–7

We then who are strong ought to bear with the scruples of the weak, and not to please ourselves. Let each of us please his neighbor for his good, leading to edification. For even Christ did not please Himself; but as it is written, "The reproaches of those who reproached You fell on Me." For whatever things were written before were written for our learning, that we through the patience and comfort of the Scriptures might have hope.

Romans 15:1–4

Therefore comfort each other and edify one another, just as you also are doing.

1 Thessalonians 5:11

Sing, O heavens!
Be joyful, O earth!
And break out in singing, O mountains!
For the LORD has comforted His people,
And will have mercy on His afflicted.
But Zion said, "The LORD has forsaken me,
And my LORD has forgotten me."
Can a woman forget her nursing child,
And not have compassion on the son of
     her womb?
Surely they may forget,
Yet I will not forget you.
See, I have inscribed you on the palms of
     My hands;
Your walls are continually before Me.

Isaiah 49:13–16

He Feels Defeated And Powerless 🍃

God is our refuge and strength,
A very present help in trouble.
Therefore we will not fear,
Even though the earth be removed,
And though the mountains be carried into
     the midst of the sea;
Though its waters roar and be troubled,
Though the mountains shake with its
     swelling.

Psalm 46:1–3

Bow down Your ear, O LORD, hear me;
For I am poor and needy.
Preserve my life, for I am holy;
You are my God;
Save Your servant who trusts in You!
Be merciful to me, O Lord,
For I cry to You all day long.
Rejoice the soul of Your servant,
For to You, O Lord, I lift up my soul.
For You, Lord, are good, and ready to forgive,
And abundant in mercy to all those who
     call upon You.
Give ear, O LORD, to my prayer;
And attend to the voice of my supplications.

Psalm 86:1–6

He who dwells in the secret place of
  the Most High
Shall abide under the shadow of
  the Almighty.
I will say of the LORD, "He is my refuge
  and my fortress;
My God, in Him I will trust."
Surely He shall deliver you from the snare
  of the fowler
And from the perilous pestilence.
He shall cover you with His feathers,
And under His wings you shall take refuge;
His truth shall be your shield and buckler.
You shall not be afraid of the terror by night,
Nor of the arrow that flies by day,
Nor of the pestilence that walks in darkness,
Nor of the destruction that lays waste at
  noonday.
A thousand may fall at your side,
And ten thousand at your right hand;
But it shall not come near you.
Only with your eyes shall you look,
And see the reward of the wicked.
Because you have made the LORD, who
  is my refuge,
Even the Most High, your dwelling place,
No evil shall befall you,
Nor shall any plague come near your
  dwelling.

Psalm 91:1–10

Trouble and anguish have overtaken me,
Yet Your commandments are my delights.
The righteousness of Your testimonies is
      everlasting;
Give me understanding, and I shall live.
Psalm 119:143–144

And those who know Your name will put
      their trust in You;
For You, LORD, have not forsaken those
      who seek You.

Psalm 9:10

I cried out to You, O LORD:
I said, "You are my refuge,
My portion in the land of the living.
Attend to my cry,
For I am brought very low;
Deliver me from my persecutors,
For they are stronger than I.
Bring my soul out of prison,
That I may praise Your name;
The righteous shall surround me,
For You shall deal bountifully with me."
Psalm 142:5–7

Give ear to my words, O LORD,
Consider my meditation.
Give heed to the voice of my cry,
My King and my God,

For to You I will pray.
My voice You shall hear in the morning,
    O LORD; ·
In the morning I will direct it to You,
And I will look up.
For You are not a God who takes pleasure in
    wickedness,
Nor shall evil dwell with You.
The boastful shall not stand in Your sight;
You hate all workers of iniquity.
You shall destroy those who speak falsehood;
The LORD abhors the bloodthirsty and
    deceitful man.
But as for me, I will come into Your house
    in the multitude of Your mercy;
In fear of You I will worship toward Your
    holy temple.
Lead me, O LORD, in Your righteousness
    because of my enemies;
Make Your way straight before my face.
But let all those rejoice who put their
    trust in You;
Let them ever shout for joy, because You
    defend them;
Let those also who love Your name
Be joyful in You.
For You, O LORD, will bless the righteous;
With favor You will surround him as with a
    shield.

Psalm 5:1–8, 11–12

Concerning this thing I pleaded with the Lord three times that it might depart from me. And He said to me, "My grace is sufficient for you, for My strength is made perfect in weakness." Therefore most gladly I will rather boast in my infirmities, that the power of Christ may rest upon me. Therefore I take pleasure in infirmities, in reproaches, in needs, in persecutions, in distresses, for Christ's sake. For when I am weak, then I am strong.

2 Corinthians 12:8–10

And I, brethren, when I came to you, did not come with excellence of speech or of wisdom declaring to you the testimony of God. For I determined not to know anything among you except Jesus Christ and Him crucified. I was with you in weakness, in fear, and in much trembling. And my speech and my preaching were not with persuasive words of human wisdom, but in demonstration of the Spirit and of power, that your faith should not be in the wisdom of men but in the power of God.

1 Corinthians 2:1–5

A Member of His Family Dies

> He heals the brokenhearted
> And binds up their wounds.
> He counts the number of the stars;
> He calls them all by name.
> Great is our Lord, and mighty in power;
> His understanding is infinite.
>
> *Psalm 147:3–5*

But I do not want you to be ignorant, brethren, concerning those who have fallen asleep, lest you sorrow as others who have no hope. For if we believe that Jesus died and rose again, even so God will bring with Him those who sleep in Jesus.

For this we say to you by the word of the Lord, that we who are alive and remain until the coming of the Lord will by no means precede those who are asleep. For the Lord Himself will descend from heaven with a shout, with the voice of an archangel, and with the trumpet of God. And the dead in Christ will rise first.

1 Thessalonians 4:13–16

> Your kingdom is an everlasting kingdom,
> And Your dominion endures throughout all
> generations.
> The LORD upholds all who fall,
> And raises up all who are bowed down.
>
> *Psalm 145:13–14*

For if the dead do not rise, then Christ is not risen. And if Christ is not risen, your faith is futile; you are still in your sins! Then also those who have fallen asleep in Christ have perished. If in this life only we have hope in Christ, we are of all men the most pitiable.

But now Christ is risen from the dead, and has become the firstfruits of those who have fallen asleep. For since by man came death, by Man also came the resurrection of the dead. For as in Adam all die, even so in Christ all shall be made alive. But each one in his own order: Christ the firstfruits, afterward those who are Christ's at His coming. Then comes the end, when He delivers the kingdom to God the Father, when He puts an end to all rule and all authority and power. For He must reign till He has put all enemies under His feet. The last enemy that will be destroyed is death.

1 Corinthians 15:16–26

For I am persuaded that neither death nor life, nor angels nor principalities nor powers, nor things present nor things to come, nor height nor depth, nor any other created thing, shall be able to separate us from the love of God which is in Christ Jesus our Lord.

Romans 8:38–39

To everything there is a season,
A time for every purpose under heaven:
    A time to be born,
And a time to die;
    A time to plant,
And a time to pluck what is planted;
    A time to kill,
And a time to heal;
    A time to break down,
And a time to build up;
    A time to weep,
And a time to laugh;
    A time to mourn,
And a time to dance;
    A time to cast away stones,
And a time to gather stones;
    A time to embrace,
And a time to refrain from embracing;
    A time to gain,
And a time to lose;
    A time to keep,
And a time to throw away;
    A time to tear,
And a time to sew;
    A time to keep silence,
And a time to speak;
    A time to love,
And a time to hate;
    A time of war,
And a time of peace.

Ecclesiastes 3:1–8

He Is Angry and Needs Peace

Behold, how good and how pleasant it is
For brethren to dwell together in unity!
It is like the precious oil upon the head,
Running down on the beard,
The beard of Aaron,
Running down on the edge of his garments.
It is like the dew of Hermon,
Descending upon the mountains of Zion;
For there the LORD commanded the
       blessing—
Life forevermore.

Psalm 133:1–3

He who is slow to wrath has great understanding,
But he who is impulsive exalts folly.

Proverbs 14:29

Better is a dinner of herbs where love is,
Than a fatted calf with hatred.
A wrathful man stirs up strife,
But he who is slow to anger allays contention.

Proverbs 15:17–18

So then, my beloved brethren, let every man
be swift to hear, slow to speak, slow to wrath; for
the wrath of man does not produce the righteousness of God.

James 1:19–20

He who is slow to anger is better than
        the mighty,
And he who rules his spirit than he who
        takes a city.

Proverbs 16:32

The beginning of strife is like releasing
        water;
Therefore stop contention before a
        quarrel starts.

Proverbs 17:14

For God is not the author of confusion but
of peace, as in all the churches of the saints.

1 Corinthians 14:33

Be angry, and do not sin: do not let the sun
go down on your wrath.

Ephesians 4:26

Let your speech always be with grace, seasoned with salt, that you may know how you
ought to answer each one.

Colossians 4:6

Now I plead with you, brethren, by the name
of our Lord Jesus Christ, that you all speak the
same thing, and that there be no divisions among
you, but that you be perfectly joined together in
the same mind and in the same judgment.

1 Corinthians 1:10

HIS LOVED ONES GROW APART

Therefore my spirit is overwhelmed
        within me;
My heart within me is distressed.
I remember the days of old;
I meditate on all Your works;
I muse on the work of Your hands.
I spread out my hands to You;
My soul longs for You like a thirsty land.
Answer me speedily, O LORD;
My spirit fails!
Do not hide Your face from me,
Lest I be like those who go down into the pit.
Cause me to hear Your lovingkindness in
        the morning,
For in You do I trust;
Cause me to know the way in which I
        should walk,
For I lift up my soul to You.

Psalm 143:4–8

He who heeds the word wisely will
        find good,
And whoever trusts in the LORD, happy is he.
Proverbs 16:20

A merry heart makes a cheerful countenance,
But by sorrow of the heart the spirit is broken.
The heart of him who has understanding
    seeks knowledge,
But the mouth of fools feeds on foolishness.
All the days of the afflicted are evil,
But he who is of a merry heart has a
    continual feast.
Better is a little with the fear of the LORD,
Than great treasure with trouble.

Proverbs 15:13–16

But Jesus knew their thoughts, and said to them: "Every kingdom divided against itself is brought to desolation, and every city or house divided against itself will not stand."

Matthew 12:25

A brother offended is harder to win than a
    strong city,
And contentions are like the bars of a castle.

Proverbs 18:19

A merry heart does good, like medicine,
But a broken spirit dries the bones.

Proverbs 17:22

Better is a dry morsel with quietness,
Than a house full of feasting with strife.

Proverbs 17:1

Pursue peace with all people, and holiness, without which no one will see the Lord: looking carefully lest anyone fall short of the grace of God; lest any root of bitterness springing up cause trouble, and by this many become defiled.

Hebrews 12:14–15

God Challenges
a Man to . . .

Grow in His Christian Walk

> Teach me, O LORD, the way of Your statutes,
> And I shall keep it to the end.
> Give me understanding, and I shall keep
>   Your law;
> Indeed, I shall observe it with my whole
>   heart.
> Make me walk in the path of Your
>   commandments,
> For I delight in it.
>
> *Psalm 119:33–35*

Now by this we know that we know Him, if we keep His commandments. He who says, "I know Him," and does not keep His commandments, is a liar, and the truth is not in him. But whoever keeps His word, truly the love of God is perfected in him. By this we know that we are in Him. He who says he abides in Him ought himself also to walk just as He walked.

1 John 2:3–6

Therefore, having these promises, beloved, let us cleanse ourselves from all filthiness of the flesh and spirit, perfecting holiness in the fear of God.

2 Corinthians 7:1

Your word is a lamp to my feet
And a light to my path.
I have sworn and confirmed
That I will keep Your righteous judgments.
I am afflicted very much;
Revive me, O LORD, according to Your
    word.
Accept, I pray, the freewill offerings of my
    mouth, O LORD,
And teach me Your judgments.
My life is continually in my hand,
Yet I do not forget Your law.

Psalm 119:105–109

Apply your heart to instruction,
And your ears to words of knowledge.

Proverbs 23:12

Teach me Your way, O LORD;
I will walk in Your truth;
Unite my heart to fear Your name.
I will praise You, O Lord my God, with all
my heart,
And I will glorify Your name forevermore.

Psalm 86:11–12

Fight the good fight of faith, lay hold on
eternal life, to which were also called and have
confessed the good confession in the presence of
many witnesses.

1 Timothy 6:12

That the righteous requirement of the law might be fulfilled in us who do not walk according to the flesh but according to the Spirit. For those who live according to the flesh set their minds on the things of the flesh, but those who live according to the Spirit, the things of the Spirit. For to be carnally minded is death, but to be spiritually minded is life and peace.

Romans 8:4–6

Two men went up to the temple to pray, one a Pharisee and the other a tax collector. The Pharisee stood and prayed thus with himself, "God, I thank You that I am not like other men—extortioners, unjust, adulterers, or even as this tax collector. I fast twice a week; I give tithes of all that I possess." And the tax collector, standing afar off, would not so much as raise his eyes to heaven, but beat his breast, saying, "God, be merciful to me a sinner!" I tell you, this man went down to his house justified rather than the other; for everyone who exalts himself will be humbled, and he who humbles himself will be exalted.

Luke 18:10–14

And do this, knowing the time, that now it is high time to awake out of sleep; for now our salvation is nearer than when we first believed. The night is far spent, the day is at hand. Therefore let us cast off the works of darkness, and let us put on the armor of light. Let us walk properly, as in the day, not in revelry and drunkenness, not in lewdness and lust, not in strife and envy. But put on the Lord Jesus Christ, and make no provision for the flesh, to fulfill its lusts.

Romans 13:11–14

Whoever believes that Jesus is the Christ is born of God, and everyone who loves Him who begot also loves him who is begotten of Him. By this we know that we love the children of God, when we love God and keep His commandments. For this is the love of God, that we keep His commandments. And His commandments are not burdensome.

1 John 5:1–3

Deal Honestly with Others

Judge not, that you be not judged. For with what judgment you judge, you will be judged; and with the measure you use, it will be measured back to you. And why do you look at the speck in your brother's eye, but do not consider the plank in your own eye? Or how can you say to your brother, "Let me remove the speck from your eye;" and look, a plank is in your own eye? Hypocrite! First remove the plank from your own eye, and then you will see clearly to remove the speck from your brother's eye.

Matthew 7:1–5

Do not lie to one another, since you have put off the old man with his deeds, and have put on the new man who is renewed in knowledge according to the image of Him who created him.

Colossians 3:9–10

Do not withhold good from those to
        whom it is due,
When it is in the power of your hand to do so.

Proverbs 3:27

Lying lips are an abomination to the LORD,
But those who deal truthfully are His delight.

Proverbs 12:22

Then the LORD sent Nathan to David. And
he came to him, and said to him: "There were two
men in one city, one rich and the other poor. The
rich man had exceedingly many flocks and herds.
But the poor man had nothing, except one little
ewe lamb which he had bought and nourished;
and it grew up together with him and with his
children. It ate of his own food and drank from his
own cup and lay in his bosom; and it was like a
daughter to him. And a traveler came to the rich
man, who refused to take from his own flock and
from his own herd to prepare one for the wayfar-
ing man who had come to him; but he took the
poor man's lamb and prepared it for the man who
had come to him."

So David's anger was greatly aroused against
the man, and he said to Nathan, "As the LORD
lives, the man who has done this shall surely die!
And he shall restore fourfold for the lamb, because
he did this thing and because he had no pity."

Then Nathan said to David, "You are the
man!"

2 Samuel 12:1–7a

And take not the word of truth utterly
   out of my mouth,
For I have hoped in Your ordinances.
So shall I keep Your law continually,
Forever and ever.
And I will walk at liberty,
For I seek Your precepts.

Psalm 119:43–45

If indeed you have heard Him and have been taught by Him, as the truth is in Jesus: that you put off, concerning your former conduct, the old man which grows corrupt according to the deceitful lusts, and be renewed in the spirit of your mind.

Ephesians 4:21–23

Ask Forgiveness of Others

A man's pride will bring him low,
But the humble in spirit will retain honor.

Proverbs 29:23

Take heed to yourselves. If your brother sins against you, rebuke him; and if he repents, forgive him. And if he sins against you seven times in a day, and seven times in a day returns to you, saying, "I repent," you shall forgive him.

Luke 17:3–4

Whenever you stand praying, if you have anything against anyone, forgive him, that your Father in heaven may also forgive you your trespasses. But if you do not forgive, neither will your Father in heaven forgive your trespasses.

Mark 11:25–26

I, therefore, the prisoner of the Lord, beseech you to walk worthy of the calling with which you were called, with all lowliness and gentleness, with longsuffering, bearing with one another in love, endeavoring to keep the unity of the Spirit in the bond of peace.

Ephesians 4:1–3

Bearing with one another, and forgiving one another, if anyone has a complaint against another; even as Christ forgave you, so you also must do.

Colossians 3:13

For if you forgive men their trespasses, your heavenly Father will also forgive you. But if you do not forgive men their trespasses, neither will your Father forgive your trespasses.

Matthew 6:14–15

Let all bitterness, wrath, anger, clamor, and evil speaking be put away from you, with all malice. And be kind to one another, tenderhearted, forgiving one another, even as God in Christ forgave you.

Ephesians 4:31–32

Repay no one evil for evil. Have regard for good things in the sight of all men. If it is possible, as much as depends on you, live peaceably with all men. Beloved, do not avenge yourselves, but rather give place to wrath; for it is written, "Vengeance is Mine, I will repay," says the Lord.

Romans 12:17–19

He who covers his sins will not prosper,
But whoever confesses and forsakes
   them will have mercy.

Proverbs 28:13

Share His Faith with Others

But what does it say? The word is near you, in your mouth and in your heart (that is, the word of faith which we preach): that if you confess with your mouth the Lord Jesus and believe in your heart that God has raised Him from the dead, you will be saved. For with the heart one believes unto righteousness, and with the mouth confession is made unto salvation. For the Scripture says, "Whoever believes on Him will not be put to shame."

Romans 10:8–11

For the equipping of the saints for the work of ministry, for the edifying of the body of Christ, till we all come to the unity of the faith and of the knowledge of the Son of God, to a perfect man, to the measure of the stature of the fullness of Christ; that we should no longer be children, tossed to and fro and carried about with every wind of doctrine, by the trickery of men, in the cunning craftiness of deceitful plotting, but, speaking the truth in love, may grow up in all things into Him who is the head—Christ.

Ephesians 4:12–15

For this is good and acceptable in the sight of God our Savior, who desires all men to be saved and to come to the knowledge of the truth.

1 Timothy 2:3–4

Brethren, if anyone among you wanders from the truth, and someone turns him back, let him know that he who turns a sinner from the error of his way will save a soul from death and cover a multitude of sins.

James 5:19–20

A woman of Samaria came to draw water. Jesus said to her, "Give Me a drink." For His disciples had gone away into the city to buy food.

John 4:7–8

Most assuredly, I say to you, he who believes in Me, the works that I do he will do also; and greater works than these he will do, because I go to My Father. And whatever you ask in My name, that I will do, that the Father may be glorified in the Son.

John 14:12–13

And let us not grow weary while doing good, for in due season we shall reap if we do not lose heart. Therefore, as we have opportunity, let us do good to all, especially to those who are of the household of faith.

Galatians 6:9–10

His lord said to him, "Well done, good and faithful servant; you were faithful over a few things, I will make you ruler over many things. Enter into the joy of your lord."

Matthew 25:21

Give, and it will be given to you: good measure, pressed down, shaken together, and running over will be put into your bosom. For with the same measure that you use, it will be measured back to you.

Luke 6:38

There is one who scatters, yet increases more;
And there is one who withholds more than
   is right,
But it leads to poverty.
The generous soul will be made rich,
And he who waters will also be watered himself.
Proverbs 11:24–25

Those who are wise shall shine
Like the brightness of the firmament,
And those who turn many to righteousness
Like the stars forever and ever.

Daniel 12:3

Be Wise with His Finances

Now it shall come to pass, if you diligently obey the voice of the LORD your God, to observe carefully all His commandments which I command you today, that the LORD your God will set you high above all nations of the earth. And all these blessings shall come upon you and overtake you, because you obey the voice of the LORD your God:

Blessed shall you be in the city, and blessed shall you be in the country.

Blessed shall be the fruit of your body, the produce of your ground and the increase of your herds, the increase of your cattle and the offspring of your flocks.

Blessed shall be your basket and your kneading bowl.

Blessed shall you be when you come in, and blessed shall you be when you go out.

Deuteronomy 28:1–6

And you shall remember the LORD your God, for it is He who gives you power to get wealth, that He may establish His covenant which He swore to your fathers, as it is this day.

Deuteronomy 8:18

Trust in the LORD, and do good;
Dwell in the land, and feed on His faithfulness.
Delight yourself also in the LORD,
And He shall give you the desires of
      your heart.
Commit your way to the LORD,
Trust also in Him,
And He shall bring it to pass.

Psalm 37:3–5

So that you do not appear to men to be fasting, but to your Father who is in the secret place; and your Father who sees in secret will reward you openly.

Do not lay up for yourselves treasures on earth, where moth and rust destroy and where thieves break in and steal; but lay up for yourselves treasures in heaven, where neither moth nor rust destroys and where thieves do not break in and steal. For where your treasure is, there your heart will be also.

Matthew 6:18–21

Then you will prosper, if you take care to fulfill the statutes and judgments with which the LORD charged Moses concerning Israel. Be strong and of good courage; do not fear nor be dismayed.

1 Chronicles 22:13

The LORD makes poor and makes rich;
He brings low and lifts up.
He raises the poor from the dust
And lifts the beggar from the ash heap,
To set them among princes
And make them inherit the throne of glory.
For the pillars of the earth are the LORD's,
And He has set the world upon them.
He will guard the feet of His saints,
But the wicked shall be silent in darkness.
For by strength no man shall prevail.

1 Samuel 2:7–9

"Bring all the tithes into the storehouse,
  That there may be food in My house,
  And try Me now in this,"
  Says the LORD of hosts,
"If I will not open for you the windows
      of heaven
  And pour out for you such blessing
  That there will not be room enough to
      receive it."

Malachi 3:10

Be Accountable to Christian Brothers 🍂

Two are better than one,
Because they have a good reward for
    their labor.
For if they fall, one will lift up his
    companion.
But woe to him who is alone when he falls,
For he has no one to help him up.

Ecclesiastes 4:9–10

Be kindly affectionate to one another with brotherly love, in honor giving preference to one another.

Romans 12:10

A man who has friends must himself
    be friendly,
But there is a friend who sticks closer than
    a brother.

Proverbs 18:24

As iron sharpens iron,
So a man sharpens the countenance of
    his friend.

Proverbs 27:17

Confess your trespasses to one another, and pray for one another, that you may be healed. The effective, fervent prayer of a righteous man avails much.

James 5:16

And if one member suffers, all the members suffer with it; or if one member is honored, all the members rejoice with it.

1 Corinthians 12:26

For now we see in a mirror, dimly, but then face to face. Now I know in part, but then I shall know just as I also am known.

1 Corinthians 13:12

Abide in Me, and I in you. As the branch cannot bear fruit of itself, unless it abides in the vine, neither can you, unless you abide in Me.

I am the vine, you are the branches. He who abides in Me, and I in him, bears much fruit; for without Me you can do nothing.

John 15:4–5

Since you have purified your souls in obeying the truth through the Spirit in sincere love of the brethren, love one another fervently with a pure heart.

1 Peter 1:22

A new commandment I give to you, that you love one another; as I have loved you, that you also love one another.

John 13:34

I, therefore, the prisoner of the Lord, beseech you to walk worthy of the calling with which you were called, with all lowliness and gentleness, with longsuffering, bearing with one another in love, endeavoring to keep the unity of the Spirit in the bond of peace.

Ephesians 4:1–3

Let each of you look out not only for his own interests, but also for the interests of others.

Philippians 2:4

Brethren, if anyone among you wanders from the truth, and someone turns him back, let him know that he who turns a sinner from the error of his way will save a soul from death and cover a multitude of sins.

James 5:19–20

Brethren, if a man is overtaken in any trespass, you who are spiritual restore such a one in a spirit of gentleness, considering yourself lest you also be tempted.

Galatians 6:1

Finally, all of you be of one mind, having compassion for one another; love as brothers, be tenderhearted, be courteous; not returning evil for evil or reviling for reviling, but on the contrary blessing, knowing that you were called to this, that you may inherit a blessing.

1 Peter 3:8–9

God Listens to a Man's Prayer When . . .

No One Else Will Listen

Ask, and it will be given to you; seek, and you will find; knock, and it will be opened to you. For everyone who asks receives, and he who seeks finds, and to him who knocks it will be opened.

Matthew 7:7–8

Continue earnestly in prayer, being vigilant in it with thanksgiving.

Colossians 4:2

Rejoicing in hope, patient in tribulation, continuing steadfastly in prayer.

Romans 12:12

Rejoice always, pray without ceasing, in everything give thanks; for this is the will of God in Christ Jesus for you.

1 Thessalonians 5:16–18

If My people who are called by My name will humble themselves, and pray and seek My face, and turn from their wicked ways, then I will hear from heaven, and will forgive their sin and heal their land.

2 Chronicles 7:14

Again I say to you that if two of you agree on earth concerning anything that they ask, it will be done for them by My Father in heaven.

Matthew 18:19

Hear a just cause, O LORD,
Attend to my cry;
Give ear to my prayer which is not
    from deceitful lips.

Psalm 17:1

Therefore take up the whole armor of God, that you may be able to withstand in the evil day, and having done all, to stand.

Stand therefore, having girded your waist with truth, having put on the breastplate of righteousness, and having shod your feet with the preparation of the gospel of peace; above all, taking the shield of faith with which you will be able to quench all the fiery darts of the wicked one. And take the helmet of salvation, and the sword of the Spirit, which is the word of God; praying always with all prayer and supplication in the Spirit, being watchful to this end with all perseverance and supplication for all the saints.

Ephesians 6:13–18

For the eyes of the LORD are on the
     righteous,
And His ears are open to their prayers;
But the face of the LORD is against those
     who do evil.

1 Peter 3:12

Hear me when I call, O God of my
     righteousness!
You have relieved me in my distress;
Have mercy on me, and hear my prayer.

Psalm 4:1

Let us therefore come boldly to the throne of
grace, that we may obtain mercy and find grace to
help in time of need.

Hebrews 4:16

So I say to you, ask, and it will be given to
you; seek, and you will find; knock, and it will be
opened to you.

Luke 11:9

He Asks for Patience

My brethren, count it all joy when you fall into various trials, knowing that the testing of your faith produces patience. But let patience have its perfect work, that you may be perfect and complete, lacking nothing.

James 1:2–4

And a servant of the Lord must not quarrel but be gentle to all, able to teach, patient.

2 Timothy 2:24

Therefore we also, since we are surrounded by so great a cloud of witnesses, let us lay aside every weight, and the sin which so easily ensnares us, and let us run with endurance the race that is set before us.

Hebrews 12:1

For even Christ did not please Himself; but as it is written, "The reproaches of those who reproached You fell on Me." For whatever things were written before were written for our learning, that we through the patience and comfort of the Scriptures might have hope. Now may the God of patience and comfort grant you to be like-minded toward one another, according to Christ Jesus.

Romans 15:3–5

Now we exhort you, brethren, warn those who are unruly, comfort the fainthearted, uphold the weak, be patient with all.

1 Thessalonians 5:14

Therefore if there is any consolation in Christ, if any comfort of love, if any fellowship of the Spirit, if any affection and mercy, fulfill my joy by being like-minded, having the same love, being of one accord, of one mind. Let nothing be done through selfish ambition or conceit, but in lowliness of mind let each esteem others better than himself. Let each of you look out not only for his own interests, but also for the interests of others.

Philippians 2:1–4

But those who wait on the LORD
Shall renew their strength;
They shall mount up with wings like eagles,
They shall run and not be weary,
They shall walk and not faint.

Isaiah 40:31

Wait on the LORD;
Be of good courage,
And He shall strengthen your heart;
Wait, I say, on the LORD!

Psalm 27:14

Rest in the LORD, and wait patiently for
    Him;
Do not fret because of him who prospers in
    his way,
Because of the man who brings wicked
    schemes to pass.
Cease from anger, and forsake wrath;
Do not fret—it only causes harm.
For evildoers shall be cut off;
But those who wait on the LORD,
They shall inherit the earth.

Psalm 37:7–9

The end of a thing is better than its beginning;
The patient in spirit is better than the
    proud in spirit.

Ecclesiastes 7:8

He Asks for Guidance from the Holy Spirit

Teach me to do Your will,
For You are my God;
Your Spirit is good.
Lead me in the land of uprightness.
Revive me, O LORD, for Your name's sake!
For Your righteousness' sake bring my
    soul out of trouble.

Psalm 143:10–11

Now the Lord is the Spirit; and where the Spirit of the Lord is, there is liberty. But we all, with unveiled face, beholding as in a mirror the glory of the Lord, are being transformed into the same image from glory to glory, just as by the Spirit of the Lord.

2 Corinthians 3:17–18

"He who believes in Me, as the Scripture has said, out of his heart will flow rivers of living water." But this He spoke concerning the Spirit, whom those believing in Him would receive; for the Holy Spirit was not yet given, because Jesus was not yet glorified.

John 7:38–39

I say then: Walk in the Spirit, and you shall not fulfill the lust of the flesh. For the flesh lusts against the Spirit, and the Spirit against the flesh; and these are contrary to one another, so that you do not do the things that you wish. But if you are led by the Spirit, you are not under the law.

Now the works of the flesh are evident, which are: adultery, fornication, uncleanness, lewdness, idolatry, sorcery, hatred, contentions, jealousies, outbursts of wrath, selfish ambitions, dissensions, heresies, envy, murders, drunkenness, revelries, and the like; of which I tell you beforehand, just as I also told you in time past, that those who practice such things will not inherit the kingdom of God.

But the fruit of the Spirit is love, joy, peace, longsuffering, kindness, goodness, faithfulness, gentleness, self-control. Against such there is no law. And those who are Christ's have crucified the flesh with its passions and desires. If we live in the Spirit, let us also walk in the Spirit. Let us not become conceited, provoking one another, envying one another.

Galatians 5:16–26

But God has revealed them to us through His Spirit. For the Spirit searches all things, yes, the deep things of God. For what man knows the things of a man except the spirit of the man which is in him? Even so no one knows the things of God except the Spirit of God. Now we have received, not the spirit of the world, but the Spirit who is from God, that we might know the things that have been freely given to us by God.

These things we also speak, not in words which man's wisdom teaches but which the Holy Spirit teaches, comparing spiritual things with spiritual. But the natural man does not receive the things of the Spirit of God, for they are foolishness to him; nor can he know them, because they are spiritually discerned. But he who is spiritual judges all things, yet he himself is rightly judged by no one. For "who has known the mind of the LORD that he may instruct Him?" But we have the mind of Christ.

1 Corinthians 2:10–16

And I will pray the Father, and He will give you another Helper, that He may abide with you forever—the Spirit of truth, whom the world cannot receive, because it neither sees Him nor knows Him; but you know Him, for He dwells with you and will be in you.

John 14:16–17

Nevertheless I tell you the truth. It is to your advantage that I go away; for if I do not go away, the Helper will not come to you; but if I depart, I will send Him to you.

However, when He, the Spirit of truth, has come, He will guide you into all truth; for He will not speak on His own authority, but whatever He hears He will speak; and He will tell you things to come.

John 16:7, 13

By this we know that we abide in Him, and He in us, because He has given us of His Spirit.

1 John 4:13

He Confesses His Sins and Seeks Forgiveness

He who covers his sins will not prosper,
But whoever confesses and forsakes them
    will have mercy.

Proverbs 28:13

The LORD is far from the wicked,
But He hears the prayer of the righteous.
The light of the eyes rejoices the heart,
And a good report makes the bones healthy.
The ear that hears the rebukes of life
Will abide among the wise.
He who disdains instruction despises his
    own soul,
But he who heeds rebuke gets understanding.
The fear of the LORD is the instruction of
    wisdom,
And before honor is humility.

Proverbs 15:29–33

If we confess our sins, He is faithful and just
to forgive us our sins and to cleanse us from all
unrighteousness.

1 John 1:9

For I will be merciful to their unrighteousness, and their sins and their lawless deeds I will remember no more.

Hebrews 8:12

Let the wicked forsake his way,
And the unrighteous man his thoughts;
Let him return to the LORD,
And He will have mercy on him;
And to our God,
For He will abundantly pardon.

Isaiah 55:7

To the praise of the glory of His grace, by which He has made us accepted in the Beloved.

In Him we have redemption through His blood, the forgiveness of sins, according to the riches of His grace.

Ephesians 1:6–7

"Come now, and let us reason together,"
  Says the LORD,
"Though your sins are like scarlet,
  They shall be as white as snow;
Though they are red like crimson,
  They shall be as wool."

Isaiah 1:18

Blessed is he whose transgression is forgiven,
Whose sin is covered.
Blessed is the man to whom the LORD does
     not impute iniquity,
And in whose spirit there is no deceit.

Psalm 32:1–2

My little children, these things I write to you, so that you may not sin. And if anyone sins, we have an Advocate with the Father, Jesus Christ the righteous.

1 John 2:1

The Responsibilities of Life Overwhelm Him 🍃

"For the mountains shall depart
And the hills be removed,
But My kindness shall not depart from you,
Nor shall My covenant of peace
   be removed,"
Says the LORD, who has mercy on you.

Isaiah 54:10

Be strong and of good courage, do not fear nor be afraid of them; for the LORD your God, He is the One who goes with you. He will not leave you nor forsake you.

Deuteronomy 31:6

Therefore, brethren, stand fast and hold the traditions which you were taught, whether by word or our epistle.

Now may our Lord Jesus Christ Himself, and our God and Father, who has loved us and given us everlasting consolation and good hope by grace, comfort your hearts and establish you in every good word and work.

2 Thessalonians 2:15–17

For I know the thoughts that I think toward you, says the LORD, thoughts of peace and not of evil, to give you a future and a hope. Then you will call upon Me and go and pray to Me, and I will listen to you. And you will seek Me and find Me, when you search for Me with all your heart.

Jeremiah 29:11–13

Unless the LORD builds the house,
They labor in vain who build it;
Unless the LORD guards the city,
The watchman stays awake in vain.
It is vain for you to rise up early,
To sit up late,
To eat the bread of sorrows;
For so He gives His beloved sleep.
Behold, children are a heritage from
   the LORD,
The fruit of the womb is a reward.
Like arrows in the hand of a warrior,
So are the children of one's youth.
Happy is the man who has his quiver full
   of them;
They shall not be ashamed,
But shall speak with their enemies in the gate.

Psalm 127:1–5

I cried out to God with my voice—
To God with my voice;
And He gave ear to me.
I remembered God, and was troubled;
I complained, and my spirit was
      overwhelmed.

Psalm 77:1, 3

Lift up your eyes on high,
And see who has created these things,
Who brings out their host by number;
He calls them all by name,
By the greatness of His might
And the strength of His power;
Not one is missing.
Why do you say, O Jacob,
And speak, O Israel:
"My way is hidden from the LORD,
And my just claim is passed over by
      my God"?
Have you not known?
Have you not heard?
The everlasting God, the LORD,
The Creator of the ends of the earth,
Neither faints nor is weary.
His understanding is unsearchable.
He gives power to the weak,
And to those who have no might
      He increases strength.

Isaiah 40:26–29

When you pass through the waters, I will
      be with you;
And through the rivers, they shall not
      overflow you.
When you walk through the fire, you
      shall not be burned,
Nor shall the flame scorch you.
Fear not, for I am with you;
I will bring your descendants from the east,
And gather you from the west;
I will say to the north, "Give them up!"
And to the south, "Do not keep them back!"
Bring My sons from afar,
And My daughters from the ends of
      the earth—
Everyone who is called by My name,
Whom I have created for My glory;
I have formed him, yes, I have made him.
Isaiah 43:2, 5–7

God Fills a Man with Joy When . . .

HE PRAISES THE Lord

I will extol You, my God, O King;
And I will bless Your name forever and ever.
Every day I will bless You,
And I will praise Your name forever and ever.
Great is the LORD, and greatly to be praised;
And His greatness is unsearchable.
One generation shall praise Your works
    to another,
And shall declare Your mighty acts.

Psalm 145:1–4

Both young men and maidens;
Old men and children.
Let them praise the name of the LORD,
For His name alone is exalted;
His glory is above the earth and heaven.
And He has exalted the horn of His people,
The praise of all His saints—
Of the children of Israel,
A people near to Him.
Praise the LORD!

Psalm 148:12–14

This people I have formed for Myself;
They shall declare My praise.

Isaiah 43:21

Praise the LORD!
Praise God in His sanctuary;
Praise Him in His mighty firmament!
Praise Him for His mighty acts;
Praise Him according to His excellent
　　　greatness!
Praise Him with the sound of the trumpet;
Praise Him with the lute and harp!
Praise Him with the timbrel and dance;
Praise Him with stringed instruments
　　　and flutes!
Praise Him with loud cymbals;
Praise Him with clashing cymbals!
Let everything that has breath praise
　　　the LORD.
Praise the LORD!

Psalm 150:1–6

I will call upon the LORD, who is worthy
　　　to be praised;
So shall I be saved from my enemies.

2 Samuel 22:4

But you are a chosen generation, a royal
priesthood, a holy nation, His own special people,
that you may proclaim the praises of Him who
called you out of darkness into His marvelous light.

1 Peter 2:9

May the LORD give you increase more
   and more,
You and your children.
May you be blessed by the LORD,
Who made heaven and earth.
The heaven, even the heavens, are
   the LORD's;
But the earth He has given to the children
   of men.
The dead do not praise the LORD,
Nor any who go down into silence.
But we will bless the LORD
From this time forth and forevermore.
Praise the LORD!

Psalm 115:14–18

Know that the LORD, He is God;
It is He who has made us, and not we ourselves;
We are His people and the sheep of His pasture.
Enter into His gates with thanksgiving,
And into His courts with praise.
Be thankful to Him, and bless His name.
For the LORD is good;
His mercy is everlasting,
And His truth endures to all generations.

Psalm 100:3–5

I will sing of the mercies of the LORD forever;
With my mouth will I make known Your
    faithfulness to all generations.
For I have said, "Mercy shall be built up
    forever;
Your faithfulness You shall establish in the
    very heavens."
"I have made a covenant with My chosen,
I have sworn to My servant David:
'Your seed I will establish forever,
And build up your throne to all generations.' "

Psalm 89:1–4

I thank You and praise You,
O God of my fathers;
You have given me wisdom and might,
And have now made known to me what we
    asked of You,
For You have made known to us the king's
    demand.

Daniel 2:23

His Children Grow to Love God 🍃

I love those who love me,
And those who seek me diligently will
find me.

Proverbs 8:17

You are the salt of the earth; but if the salt loses its flavor, how shall it be seasoned? It is then good for nothing but to be thrown out and trampled underfoot by men.

You are the light of the world. A city that is set on a hill cannot be hidden. Nor do they light a lamp and put it under a basket, but on a lampstand, and it gives light to all who are in the house. Let your light so shine before men, that they may see your good works and glorify your Father in heaven.

Matthew 5:13–16

That Christ may dwell in your hearts through faith; that you, being rooted and grounded in love, may be able to comprehend with all the saints what is the width and length and depth and height— to know the love of Christ which passes knowledge; that you may be filled with all the fullness of God.

Ephesians 3:17–19

"At the same time," says the LORD, "I will be the God of all the families of Israel, and they shall be My people."

Thus says the LORD:
"The people who survived the sword
Found grace in the wilderness—
Israel, when I went to give him rest."
The LORD has appeared of old to me, saying:
"Yes, I have loved you with an everlasting
     love;
Therefore with lovingkindness I have drawn
     you."

Jeremiah 31:1–3

And you shall love the LORD your God with all your heart, with all your soul, with all your mind, and with all your strength. This is the first commandment.

Mark 12:30

As the Father loved Me, I also have loved you; abide in My love. If you keep My commandments, you will abide in My love, just as I have kept My Father's commandments and abide in His love.

John 15:9–10

He Worships God

Then we cried out to the LORD God of our fathers, and the LORD heard our voice and looked on our affliction and our labor and our oppression. So the LORD brought us out of Egypt with a mighty hand and with an outstretched arm, with great terror and with signs and wonders. He has brought us to this place and has given us this land, a land flowing with milk and honey; and now, behold, I have brought the firstfruits of the land which you, O LORD, have given me. Then you shall set it before the LORD your God, and worship before the LORD your God.

Deuteronomy 26:7–10

Also with the lute I will praise you—
And Your faithfulness, O my God!
To You I will sing with the harp,
O Holy One of Israel.
My lips shall greatly rejoice when I sing
    to You,
And my soul, which You have redeemed.
My tongue also shall talk of Your
    righteousness all the day long;
For they are confounded,
For they are brought to shame
Who seek my hurt.

Psalm 71:22–24

The LORD lives!
Blessed be my Rock!
Let God be exalted,
The Rock of my salvation!

2 Samuel 22:47

Make a joyful shout to the LORD, all
you lands!
Serve the LORD with gladness;
Come before His presence with singing.

Psalm 100:1–2

Then Jesus said to him, "Away with you,
Satan! For it is written, 'You shall worship the
Lord your God, and Him only you shall serve.'"

Matthew 4:10

Let them give glory to the LORD,
And declare His praise in the coastlands.

Isaiah 42:12

Let the word of Christ dwell in you richly in
all wisdom, teaching and admonishing one another
in psalms and hymns and spiritual songs, singing
with grace in your hearts to the Lord.

Colossians 3:16

Give to the LORD the glory due His name;
Bring an offering, and come before Him.
Oh, worship the LORD in the beauty of holiness!

1 Chronicles 16:29

God Keeps a Man
Secure When . . .

He Puts God First in His Life

Therefore humble yourselves under the mighty hand of God, that He may exalt you in due time, casting all your cate upon Him, for He cares for you.

1 Peter 5:6–7

My son, if you receive my words,
And treasure my commands within you,
So that you incline your ear to wisdom,
And apply your heart to understanding;
Yes, if you cry out for discernment,
And lift up your voice for understanding,
If you seek her as silver,
And search for her as for hidden treasures;
Then you will understand the fear of
     the LORD,
And find the knowledge of God.

Proverbs 2:1–5

Be strong and of good courage, do not fear nor be afraid of them; for the LORD your God, He is the One who goes with you. He will not leave you nor forsake you.

Deuteronomy 31:6

Then the king arose very early in the morning and went in haste to the den of lions. And when he came to the den, he cried out with a lamenting voice to Daniel. The king spoke, saying to Daniel, "Daniel, servant of the living God, has your God, whom you serve continually, been able to deliver you from the lions?"

Then Daniel said to the king, "O king, live forever! My God sent His angel and shut the lions' mouths, so that they have not hurt me, because I was found innocent before Him; and also, O king, I have done no wrong before you."

Daniel 6:19–22

I will love You, O LORD, my strength.
The LORD is my rock and my fortress
and my deliverer;
My God, my strength, in whom I will trust;
My shield and the horn of my salvation,
my stronghold.
I will call upon the LORD, who is worthy
to be praised;
So shall I be saved from my enemies.

Psalm 18:1–3

Therefore submit to God. Resist the devil and he will flee from you. Draw near to God and He will draw near to you. Cleanse your hands, you sinners; and purify your hearts, you double-minded.

James 4:7–8

This Book of the Law shall not depart from your mouth, but you shall meditate in it day and night, that you may observe to do according to all that is written in it. For then you will make your way prosperous, and then you will have good success. Have I not commanded you? Be strong and of good courage; do not be afraid, nor be dismayed, for the LORD your God is with you wherever you go.

Joshua 1:8–9

When wisdom enters your heart,
And knowledge is pleasant to your soul,
Discretion will preserve you;
Understanding will keep you,
To deliver you from the way of evil,
From the man who speaks perverse things.
Proverbs 2:10–12

He Makes a Major Job Change

For the Scripture says, "You shall not muzzle an ox while it treads out the grain," and, "The laborer is worthy of his wages."

1 Timothy 5:18

What profit has the worker from that in which he labors? I have seen the God-given task with which the sons of men are to be occupied. He has made everything beautiful in its time. Also He has put eternity in their hearts, except that no one can find out the work that God does from beginning to end.

I know that nothing is better for them than to rejoice, and to do good in their lives, and also that every man should eat and drink and enjoy the good of all his labor—it is the gift of God.

Ecclesiastes 3:9–13

Do not overwork to be rich;
Because of your own understanding, cease!
Will you set your eyes on that which is not?
For riches certainly make themselves wings;
They fly away like an eagle toward heaven.

Proverbs 23:4–5

Then I hated all my labor in which I had toiled under the sun, because I must leave it to the man who will come after me. And who knows whether he will be wise or a fool? Yet he will rule over all my labor in which I toiled and in which I have shown myself wise under the sun. This also is vanity. Therefore I turned my heart and despaired of all the labor in which I had toiled under the sun.

For God gives wisdom and knowledge and joy to a man who is good in His sight; but to the sinner He gives the work of gathering and collecting, that he may give to him who is good before God. This also is vanity and grasping for the wind.

Ecclesiastes 2:18–20, 26

For no other foundation can anyone lay than that which is laid, which is Jesus Christ. Now if anyone builds on this foundation with gold, silver, precious stones, wood, hay, straw, each one's work will become clear; for the Day will declare it, because it will be revealed by fire; and the fire will test each one's work, of what sort it is. If anyone's work which he has built on it endures, he will receive a reward. If anyone's work is burned, he will suffer loss; but he himself will be saved, yet so as through fire.

1 Corinthians 3:11–15

Therefore I say to you, do not worry about your life, what you will eat or what you will drink; nor about your body, what you will put on. Is not life more than food and the body more than clothing? Look at the birds of the air, for they neither sow nor reap nor gather into barns; yet your heavenly Father feeds them. Are you not of more value than they? Which of you by worrying can add one cubit to his stature?

So why do you worry about clothing? Consider the lilies of the field, how they grow: they neither toil nor spin; and yet I say to you that even Solomon in all his glory was not arrayed like one of these. Now if God so clothes the grass of the field, which today is, and tomorrow is thrown into the oven, will He not much more clothe you, O you of little faith?

Therefore do not worry, saying, "What shall we eat?" or "What shall we drink?" or "What shall we wear?" For after all these things the Gentiles seek. For your heavenly Father knows that you need all these things. But seek first the kingdom of God and His righteousness, and all these things shall be added to you. Therefore do not worry about tomorrow, for tomorrow will worry about its own things. Sufficient for the day is its own trouble.

Matthew 6:25–34

The name of the LORD is a strong tower;
The righteous run to it and are safe.

Proverbs 18:10

Do not put your trust in princes,
Nor in a son of man, in whom there is
    no help.
His spirit departs, he returns to his earth;
In that very day his plans perish.
Happy is he who has the God of Jacob for
    his help,
Whose hope is in the LORD his God.

Psalm 146:3–5

Worry and Doubt Threaten His Well-Being 🍃

You will keep him in perfect peace,
Whose mind is stayed on You,
Because he trusts in You.

Isaiah 26:3

The eyes of all look expectantly to You,
And You give them their food in due season.
You open Your hand
And satisfy the desire of every living thing.
The LORD is righteous in all His ways,
Gracious in all His works.
The LORD is near to all who call upon Him,
To all who call upon Him in truth.
He will fulfill the desire of those who fear Him;
He also will hear their cry and save them.
The LORD preserves all who love Him,
But all the wicked He will destroy.
My mouth shall speak the praise of the LORD,
And all flesh shall bless His holy name
Forever and ever.

Psalm 145:15–21

The work of righteousness will be peace,
And the effect of righteousness, quietness
      and assurance forever.

Isaiah 32:17

I will both lie down in peace, and sleep;
For You alone, O LORD, make me dwell
    in safety.

Psalm 4:8

Blessed is every one who fears the LORD,
Who walks in His ways.
When you eat the labor of your hands,
You shall be happy, and it shall be well
    with you.
Your wife shall be like a fruitful vine
In the very heart of your house,
Your children like olive plants
All around your table.
Behold, thus shall the man be blessed
Who fears the LORD.
The LORD bless you out of Zion,
And may you see the good of Jerusalem
All the days of your life.
Yes, may you see your children's children.
Peace be upon Israel!

Psalm 128:1–6

For I will pour water on him who is thirsty,
And floods on the dry ground;
I will pour My Spirit on your descendants,
And My blessing on your offspring.

Isaiah 44:3

But because the LORD loves you, and because He would keep the oath which He swore to your fathers, the LORD has brought you out with a mighty hand, and redeemed you from the house of bondage, from the hand of Pharaoh king of Egypt.

Therefore know that the LORD your God, He is God, the faithful God who keeps covenant and mercy for a thousand generations with those who love Him and keep His commandments.

Deuteronomy 7:8–9

Your mercy, O LORD, is in the heavens;
Your faithfulness reaches to the clouds.

Psalm 36:5

Blessed be the LORD,
Who daily loads us with benefits,
The God of our salvation!

Psalm 68:19

The father of the righteous will greatly
    rejoice,
And he who begets a wise child will
    delight in him.
Let your father and your mother be glad,
And let her who bore you rejoice.
My son, give me your heart,
And let your eyes observe my ways.

Proverbs 23:24–26

He Doesn't Have Money to Pay the Bills 🍃

> The young lions lack and suffer hunger;
> But those who seek the LORD shall not
> lack any good thing.
>
> *Psalm 34:10*

> The humble shall see this and be glad;
> And you who seek God, your hearts shall live.
> For the LORD hears the poor,
> And does not despise His prisoners.
> Let heaven and earth praise Him,
> The seas and everything that moves in them.
>
> *Psalm 69:32–34*

The LORD will command the blessing on you in your storehouses and in all to which you set your hand, and He will bless you in the land which the LORD your God is giving you.

Deuteronomy 28:8

> The poor and needy seek water, but there
> is none,
> Their tongues fail for thirst.
> I, the LORD, will hear them;
> I, the God of Israel, will not forsake them.
>
> *Isaiah 41:17*

Come to the waters;
And you who have no money,
Come, buy and eat.
Yes, come, buy wine and milk
Without money and without price.
Why do you spend money for what is
    . not bread,
And your wages for what does not satisfy?
Listen carefully to Me, and eat what is good,
And let your soul delight itself in abundance.
Incline your ear, and come to Me.
Hear, and your soul shall live;
And I will make an everlasting covenant
    with you—
The sure mercies of David.

Isaiah 55:1–3

I have been young, and now am old;
Yet I have not seen the righteous forsaken,
Nor his descendants begging bread.
He is ever merciful, and lends;
And his descendants are blessed.
Depart from evil, and do good;
And dwell forevermore.
For the LORD loves justice,
And does not forsake His saints;
They are preserved forever,
But the descendants of the wicked shall
    be cut off.

Psalm 37:25–28

You shall eat in plenty and be satisfied,
And praise the name of the LORD your God,
Who has dealt wondrously with you;
And My people shall never be put to shame.

Joel 2:26

And my God shall supply all your need
according to His riches in glory by Christ Jesus.

Philippians 4:19

I will satiate the soul of the priests with
    abundance,
And My people shall be satisfied with My
    goodness, says the LORD.

Jeremiah 31:14

God Comforts a Man When . . .

He Feels Inadequate for His Responsibilities 🍂

For the LORD God will help Me;
Therefore I will not be disgraced;
Therefore I have set My face like a flint,
And I know that I will not be ashamed.

Isaiah 50:7

Come to Me, all you who labor and are heavy laden, and I will give you rest. Take My yoke upon you and learn from Me, for I am gentle and lowly in heart, and you will find rest for your souls. For My yoke is easy and My burden is light.

Matthew 11:28–30

For the eyes of the LORD run to and fro throughout the whole earth, to show Himself strong on behalf of those whose heart is loyal to Him.

2 Chronicles 16:9

"I will be a Father to you, and you shall be My sons and daughters," says the Lord Almighty.

2 Corinthians 6:18

Not that we are sufficient of ourselves to think of anything as being from ourselves, but our sufficiency is from God.

2 Corinthians 3:5

LORD, my heart is not haughty,
Nor my eyes lofty.
Neither do I concern myself with great matters,
Nor with things too profound for me.
Surely I have calmed and quieted my soul,
Like a weaned child with his mother;
Like a weaned child is my soul within me.
O Israel, hope in the LORD
From this time forth and forever.

Psalm 131:1–3

But by the grace of God I am what I am, and His grace toward me was not in vain; but I labored more abundantly than they all, yet not I, but the grace of God which was with me. Therefore, whether it was I or they, so we preach and so you believed.

1 Corinthians 15:10–11

I have blotted out, like a thick cloud,
  your transgressions,
And like a cloud, your sins.
Return to Me, for I have redeemed you.

Isaiah 44:22

By which have been given to us exceedingly great and precious promises, that through these you may be partakers of the divine nature, having escaped the corruption that is in the world through lust.

But also for this very reason, giving all diligence, add to your faith virtue, to virtue knowledge, to knowledge self-control, to self-control perseverance, to perseverance godliness, to godliness brotherly kindness, and to brotherly kindness love. For if these things are yours and abound, you will be neither barren nor unfruitful in the knowledge of our Lord Jesus Christ.

2 Peter 1:4–8

His Loved Ones Are Ill

Beloved, I pray that you may prosper in all things and be in health, just as your soul prospers.

3 John 2

Jesus said to him, "If you can believe, all things are possible to him who believes."

Immediately the father of the child cried out and said with tears, "Lord, I believe; help my unbelief!"

Mark 9:23–24

When Jesus came into the ruler's house, and saw the flute players and the noisy crowd wailing, He said to them, "Make room, for the girl is not dead, but sleeping." And they ridiculed Him. But when the crowd was put outside, He went in and took her by the hand, and the girl arose. And the report of this went out into all that land.

Matthew 9:23–26

But He was wounded for our transgressions,
He was bruised for our iniquities;
The chastisement for our peace was
    upon Him,
And by His stripes we are healed.

Isaiah 53:5

Is anyone among you sick? Let him call for the elders of the church, and let them pray over him, anointing him with oil in the name of the Lord. And the prayer of faith will save the sick, and the Lord will raise him up. And if he has committed sins, he will be forgiven. Confess your trespasses to one another, and pray for one another, that you may be healed. The effective, fervent prayer of a righteous man avails much.

James 5:14–16

Who Himself bore our sins in His own body on the tree, that we, having died to sins, might live for righteousness—by whose stripes you were healed.

1 Peter 2:24

Heal me, O LORD, and I shall be healed;
Save me, and I shall be saved,
For You are my praise.

Jeremiah 17:14

"For I will restore health to you
And heal you of your wounds," says
the LORD.

Jeremiah 30:17a

If you diligently heed the voice of the LORD your God and do what is right in His sight, give ear to His commandments and keep all His statutes, I will put none of the diseases on you which I have brought on the Egyptians. For I am the LORD who heals you.

Exodus 15:26

My son, give attention to my words;
Incline your ear to my sayings.
Do not let them depart from your eyes;
Keep them in the midst of your heart;
For they are life to those who find them,
And health to all their flesh.

Proverbs 4:20–22

His Loved Ones Don't Understand Him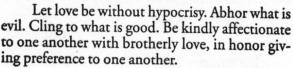

Let love be without hypocrisy. Abhor what is evil. Cling to what is good. Be kindly affectionate to one another with brotherly love, in honor giving preference to one another.

Romans 12:9–10

A word fitly spoken is like apples of gold
In settings of silver.
By long forbearance a ruler is persuaded,
And a gentle tongue breaks a bone.

Proverbs 25:11, 15

Though I speak with the tongues of men and of angels, but have not love, I have become sounding brass or a clanging cymbal. And though I have the gift of prophecy, and understand all mysteries and all knowledge, and though I have all faith, so that I could remove mountains, but have not love, I am nothing. And though I bestow all my goods to feed the poor, and though I give my body to be burned, but have not love, it profits me nothing.

1 Corinthians 13:1–3

Great is our LORD, and mighty in power; His understanding is infinite.

Psalm 147:5

For if you love those who love you, what reward have you? Do not even the tax collectors do the same? And if you greet your brethren only, what do you do more than others? Do not even the tax collectors do so? Therefore you shall be perfect, just as your Father in heaven is perfect.

Matthew 5:46–48

Finally, all of you be of one mind, having compassion for one another; love as brothers, be tenderhearted, be courteous; not returning evil for evil or reviling for reviling, but on the contrary blessing, knowing that you were called to this, that you may inherit a blessing. For
"He who would love life
And see good days,
Let him refrain his tongue from evil,
And his lips from speaking deceit.
Let him turn away from evil and do good;
Let him seek peace and pursue it."

1 Peter 3:8–11

He Must Discipline His Loved Ones 🍂

My son, do not despise the chastening of
   the LORD,
Nor detest His correction;
For whom the LORD loves He corrects,
Just as a father the son in whom he delights.
                                    Proverbs 3:11–12

Furthermore, we have had human fathers
who corrected us, and we paid them respect. Shall
we not much more readily be in subjection to the
Father of spirits and live? For they indeed for a few
days chastened us as seemed best to them, but He
for our profit, that we may be partakers of His
holiness. Now no chastening seems to be joyful for
the present, but painful; nevertheless, afterward it
yields the peaceable fruit of righteousness to those
who have been trained by it.

                                    Hebrews 12:9–11

The rod and rebuke give wisdom,
But a child left to himself brings shame to
   his mother.
Correct your son, and he will give you rest;
Yes, he will give delight to your soul.
                                    Proverbs 29:15, 17

Now I rejoice, not that you were made sorry, but that your sorrow led to repentance. For you were made sorry in a godly manner, that you might suffer loss from us in nothing.

2 Corinthians 7:9

Chasten your son while there is hope,
And do not set your heart on his destruction.
Proverbs 19:18

Hatred stirs up strife,
But love covers all sins.
Wisdom is found on the lips of him who
has understanding,
But a rod is for the back of him who
is devoid of understanding.
Proverbs 10:12–13

Whoever loves instruction loves knowledge,
But he who hates correction is stupid.
A good man obtains favor from the LORD,
But a man of wicked intentions He will
condemn.
A man is not established by wickedness,
But the root of the righteous cannot
be moved.
Proverbs 12:1–3

Therefore be very courageous to keep and to do all that is written in the Book of the Law of Moses, lest you turn aside from it to the right hand or to the left, . . .

But you shall hold fast to the LORD your God, as you have done to this day.

Joshua 23:6, 8

My son, keep my words,
And treasure my commands within you.
Keep my commands and live,
And my law as the apple of your eye.
Bind them on your fingers;
Write them on the tablet of your heart.

Proverbs 7:1–3

He Feels Powerless to Shield His Loved Ones from Evil 🍃

My son, if you receive my words,
And treasure my commands within you,
So that you incline your ear to wisdom,
And apply your heart to understanding;
Yes, if you cry out for discernment,
And lift up your voice for understanding,
If you seek her as silver,
And search for her as for hidden treasures;
Then you will understand the fear of
   the LORD,
And find the knowledge of God.
For the LORD gives wisdom;
From His mouth come knowledge
   and understanding;
He stores up sound wisdom for the upright;
He is a shield to those who walk uprightly;
He guards the paths of justice,
And preserves the way of His saints.
Then you will understand righteousness
   and justice,
Equity and every good path.

Proverbs 2:1–9

In the fear of the LORD there is strong
    confidence,
And His children will have a place of refuge.
The fear of the LORD is a fountain of life,
To turn one away from the snares of death.

Proverbs 14:26–27

In the way of righteousness is life,
And in its pathway there is no death.

Proverbs 12:28

Wine is a mocker,
Strong drink is a brawler,
And whoever is led astray by it is not wise.

Proverbs 20:1

He who loves pleasure will be a poor man;
He who loves wine and oil will not be rich.

Proverbs 21:17

In mercy and truth
Atonement is provided for iniquity;
And by the fear of the LORD one departs
    from evil.

Proverbs 16:6

Do you not know that you are the temple of God and that the Spirit of God dwells in you? If anyone defiles the temple of God, God will destroy him. For the temple of God is holy, which temple you are.

1 Corinthians 3:16–17

And do not fear those who kill the body but cannot kill the soul. But rather fear Him who is able to destroy both soul and body in hell.

Matthew 10:28

God's Love Is with a Man When . . .

He Brings His Problems to God

If you would prepare your heart,
And stretch out your hands toward Him;
If iniquity were in your hand, and you put
    it far away,
And would not let wickedness dwell in
        your tents;
Then surely you could lift up your face
        without spot;
Yes, you could be steadfast, and not fear;
Because you would forget your misery,
And remember it as waters that have
        passed away,
And your life would be brighter than
        noonday.
Though you were dark, you would be
    like the morning.
And you would be secure, because there
    is hope;
Yes, you would dig around you, and
    take your rest in safety.

Job 11:13–18

But Jesus looked at them and said to them,
"With men this is impossible, but with God all
things are possible."

Matthew 19:26

Blessed be the LORD, who has given rest to His people Israel, according to all that He promised. There has not failed one word of all His good promise, which He promised through His servant Moses. May the LORD our God be with us, as He was with our fathers. May He not leave us nor forsake us, that He may incline our hearts to Himself, to walk in all His ways, and to keep His commandments and His statutes and His judgments, which He commanded our fathers. And may these words of mine, with which I have made supplication before the LORD, be near the LORD our God day and night, that He may maintain the cause of His servant and the cause of His people Israel, as each day may require.

1 Kings 8:56–59

For the eyes of the LORD are on the righteous,
And His ears are open to their prayers;
But the face of the LORD is against those
    who do evil.
And who is he who will harm you if you become followers of what is good? But even if you should suffer for righteousness' sake, you are blessed. And do not be afraid of their threats, nor be troubled. But sanctify the Lord God in your hearts, and always be ready to give a defense to everyone who asks you a reason for the hope that is in you, with meekness and fear.

1 Peter 3:12–15

And to give you who are troubled rest with us when the Lord Jesus is revealed from heaven with His mighty angels, in flaming fire taking vengeance on those who do not know God, and on those who do not obey the gospel of our Lord Jesus Christ. These shall be punished with everlasting destruction from the presence of the Lord and from the glory of His power, when He comes, in that Day, to be glorified in His saints and to be admired among all those who believe, because our testimony among you was believed.

Therefore we also pray always for you that our God would count you worthy of this calling, and fulfill all the good pleasure of His goodness and the work of faith with power, that the name of our Lord Jesus Christ may be glorified in you, and you in Him, according to the grace of our God and the Lord Jesus Christ.

2 Thessalonians 1:7–12

Yes, we had the sentence of death in ourselves, that we should not trust in ourselves but in God who raises the dead, who delivered us from so great a death, and does deliver us; in whom we trust that He will still deliver us.

2 Corinthians 1:9–10

The Spirit of the Lord GOD is upon Me,
Because the LORD has anointed Me
To preach good tidings to the poor;
He has sent Me to heal the brokenhearted,
To proclaim liberty to the captives,
And the opening of the prison to those
    who are bound;
To proclaim the acceptable year of the LORD,
And the day of vengeance of our God;
To comfort all who mourn,
To console those who mourn in Zion,
To give them beauty for ashes,
The oil of joy for mourning,
The garment of praise for the spirit
    of heaviness;
That they may be called trees of righteousness,
The planting of the LORD, that He may
    be glorified.

Isaiah 61:1–3

God is my strength and power, and He makes
my way perfect.

2 Samuel 22:33

In Your hand is power and might; in Your
hand it is to make great and to give strength to all.

1 Chronicles 29:12

Now thanks be to God who always leads us in triumph in Christ, and through us diffuses the fragrance of His knowledge in every place. For we are to God the fragrance of Christ among those being saved and among those who are perishing. To the one we are the aroma of death leading to death, and to the other the aroma of life leading to life. And who is sufficient for these things? For we are not, as so many, peddling the word of God; but as of sincerity, but as from God we speak in the sight of God in Christ.

2 Corinthians 2:14–17

Consider what I say, and may the Lord give you understanding in all things. This is a faithful saying:
For if we died with Him,
We shall also live with Him.
If we endure,
We shall also reign with Him.
If we deny Him,
He also will deny us.

2 Timothy 2:7, 11–12

You have made the heavens and the earth by Your great power and outstreached arm. There is nothing too hard for You.

Jeremiah 32:17

We are hard pressed on every side, yet not crushed; we are perplexed, but not in despair; persecuted, but not forsaken; struck down, but not destroyed—always carrying about in the body the dying of the Lord Jesus, that the life of Jesus also may be manifested in our body.

For all things are for your sakes, that grace, having spread through the many, may cause thanksgiving to abound to the glory of God.

Therefore we do not lose heart. Even though our outward man is perishing, yet the inward man is being renewed day by day. For our light affliction, which is but for a moment, is working for us a far more exceeding and eternal weight of glory, while we do not look at the things which are seen, but at the things which are not seen. For the things which are seen are temporary, but the things which are not seen are eternal.

2 Corinthians 4;8–10, 15–18

He Relies on God to Guide His Life

My little children, these things I write to you, so that you may not sin. And if anyone sins, we have an Advocate with the Father, Jesus Christ the righteous.

1 John 2:1

The Son of Man has come to seek and to save that which was lost.

Luke 19:10

Have you not known?
Have you not heard?
The everlasting God, the LORD,
The Creator of the ends of the earth,
Neither faints nor is weary.
His understanding is unsearchable.
He gives power to the weak,
And to those who have no might He
    increases strength.
Even the youths shall faint and be weary,
And the young men shall utterly fall,
But those who wait on the LORD
Shall renew their strength;
They shall mount up with wings like eagles,
They shall run and not be weary,
They shall walk and not faint.

Isaiah 40:28–31

When you roam, they will lead you;
When you sleep, they will keep you;
And when you awake, they will speak
    with you.
For the commandment is a lamp,
And the law a light;
Reproofs of instruction are the way of life.

Proverbs 6:22–23

I will go before you
And make the crooked places straight;
I will break in pieces the gates of bronze
And cut the bars of iron.
I will give you the treasures of darkness
And hidden riches of secret places,
That you may know that I, the LORD,
Who call you by your name,
Am the God of Israel.

Isaiah 45:2–3

Do not remember the former things,
Nor consider the things of old.
Behold, I will do a new thing,
Now it shall spring forth;
Shall you not know it?
I will even make a road in the wilderness
And rivers in the desert.

Isaiah 43:18–19

Fear not, for I am with you;
Be not dismayed, for I am your God.
I will strengthen you,
Yes, I will help you,
I will uphold you with My righteous
    right hand.

Isaiah 41:10

For as the rain comes down, and the
    snow from heaven,
And do not return there,
But water the earth,
And make it bring forth and bud,
That it may give seed to the sower
And bread to the eater,
So shall My word be that goes forth from
    My mouth;
It shall not return to Me void,
But it shall accomplish what I please,
And it shall prosper in the thing for which
    I sent it.

Isaiah 55:10–11

You have been my defense and refuge in the
day of my trouble.

Psalm 59:16

"I have made the earth,
And created man on it.
I—My hands— stretched out the heavens,
And all their host I have commanded.
I have raised him up in righteousness,
And I will direct all his ways;
He shall build My city
And let My exiles go free,
Not for price nor reward,"
Says the LORD of hosts.

Isaiah 45:12–13

"For the mountains shall depart
And the hills be removed,
But My kindness shall not depart from you,
Nor shall My covenant of peace
be removed,"
Says the LORD, who has mercy on you.

Isaiah 54:10

He Shares His Good Fortune with Others 🍂

You shall surely give to him, and your heart should not be grieved when you give to him, because for this thing the LORD your God will bless you in all your works and in all to which you put your hand. For the poor will never cease from the land; therefore I command you, saying, "You shall open your hand wide to your brother, to your poor and your needy, in your land."

Deuteronomy 15:10–11

The LORD makes poor and makes rich;
He brings low and lifts up.
He raises the poor from the dust
And lifts the beggar from the ash heap,
To set them among princes
And make them inherit the throne of glory.
For the pillars of the earth are the LORD's,
And He has set the world upon them.

1 Samuel 2:7–8

Give, and it will be given to you: good measure, pressed down, shaken together, and running over will be put into your bosom.

Luke 6:38

He who oppresses the poor reproaches
    his Maker,
But he who honors Him has mercy on
    the needy.

Proverbs 14:31

Now the multitude of those who believed were of one heart and one soul; neither did anyone say that any of the things he possessed was his own, but they had all things in common. And with great power the apostles gave witness to the resurrection of the LORD Jesus. And great grace was upon them all. Nor was there anyone among them who lacked; for all who were possessors of lands or houses sold them, and brought the proceeds of the things that were sold, and laid them at the apostles' feet; and they distributed to each as anyone had need.

Acts 4:32–35

He who mocks the poor reproaches
    his Maker;
He who is glad at calamity will not
    go unpunished.

Proverbs 17:5

It is more blessed to give than to receive.
Acts 20:35

What does it profit, my brethren, if someone says he has faith but does not have works? Can faith save him? If a brother or sister is naked and destitute of daily food, and one of you says to them, "Depart in peace, be warmed and filled," but you do not give them the things which are needed for the body, what does it profit? Thus also faith by itself, if it does not have works, is dead.

James 2:14–17

Jesus said to him, "If you want to be perfect, go, sell what you have and give to the poor, and you will have treasure in heaven; and come, follow Me."

But when the young man heard that saying, he went away sorrowful, for he had great possessions.

Then Jesus said to His disciples, "Assuredly, I say to you that it is hard for a rich man to enter the kingdom of heaven. And again I say to you, it is easier for a camel to go through the eye of a needle than for a rich man to enter the kingdom of God."

Matthew 19:21–24

He Prays with His Family

Delight yourself also in the LORD,
And He shall give you the desires of
your heart.

Psalm 37:4

The LORD is near to all who call upon Him,
To all who call upon Him in truth.
He will fulfill the desire of those who
fear Him;
He also will hear their cry and save them.

Psalm 145:18–19

Rejoice in the Lord always. Again I will say, rejoice!

Let your gentleness be known to all men. The Lord is at hand.

Be anxious for nothing, but in everything by prayer and supplication, with thanksgiving, let your requests be made known to God; and the peace of God, which surpasses all understanding, will guard your hearts and minds through Christ Jesus.

Philippians 4:4–7

Call to Me, and I will answer you, and show you great and mighty things, which you do not know.

Jeremiah 33:3

You also helping together in prayer for us, that thanks may be given by many persons on our behalf for the gift granted to us through many.

For our boasting is this: the testimony of our conscience that we conducted ourselves in the world in simplicity and godly sincerity, not with fleshly wisdom but by the grace of God, and more abundantly toward you. For we are not writing any other things to you than what you read or understand. Now I trust you will understand, even to the end (as also you have understood us in part), that we are your boast as you also are ours, in the day of the Lord Jesus.

2 Corinthians 1:11–14

And whatever things you ask in prayer, believing, you will receive.

Matthew 21:22

Again I say to you that if two of you agree on earth concerning anything that they ask, it will be done for them by My Father in heaven. For where two or three are gathered together in My name, I am there in the midst of them.

Matthew 18:19–20

Let us therefore come boldly to the throne of grace, that we may obtain mercy and find grace to help in time of need.

Hebrews 4:16

Then I set my face toward the Lord God to make request by prayer and supplications, with fasting, sackcloth, and ashes. And I prayed to the LORD my God, and made confession, and said, "O Lord, great and awesome God, who keeps His covenant and mercy with those who love Him, and with those who keep His commandments, we have sinned and committed iniquity, we have done wickedly and rebelled, even by departing from Your precepts and Your judgments."

"Now therefore, our God, hear the prayer of Your servant, and his supplications, and for the Lord's sake cause Your face to shine on Your sanctuary, which is desolate. O my God, incline Your ear and hear; open Your eyes and see our desolations, and the city which is called by Your name; for we do not present our supplications before You because of our righteous deeds, but because of Your great mercies."

Daniel 9:3–5, 17–18

He Forgives Those Who Have Offenced Him 🍂

Then Peter came to Him and said, "Lord, how often shall my brother sin against me, and I forgive him? Up to seven times?"

Jesus said to him, "I do not say to you, up to seven times, but up to seventy times seven."

Matthew 18:21–22

He made known His ways to Moses,
His acts to the children of Israel.
The LORD is merciful and gracious,
Slow to anger, and abounding in mercy.
He will not always strive with us,
Nor will He keep His anger forever.
He has not dealt with us according to
    our sins,
Nor punished us according to our iniquities.
For as the heavens are high above the earth,
So great is His mercy toward those who
    fear Him;
As far as the east is from the west,
So far has He removed our transgressions
    from us.
As a father pities his children,
So the LORD pities those who fear Him.

Psalm 103:7–13

Take heed to yourselves. If your brother sins against you, rebuke him; and if he repents, forgive him. And if he sins against you seven times in a day, and seven times in a day returns to you, saying, "I repent" you shall forgive him."

Luke 17:3–4

But love your enemies, do good, and lend, hoping for nothing in return; and your reward will be great, and you will be sons of the Most High. For He is kind to the unthankful and evil. Therefore be merciful, just as your Father also is merciful.

Judge not, and you shall not be judged. Condemn not, and you shall not be condemned. Forgive, and you will be forgiven.

Luke 6:35–37

For if you forgive men their trespasses, your heavenly Father will also forgive you. But if you do not forgive men their trespasses, neither will your Father forgive your trespasses.

Matthew 6:14–15

Whenever you stand praying, if you have anything against anyone, forgive him, that your Father in heaven may also forgive you your trespasses. But if you do not forgive, neither will your Father in heaven forgive your trespasses.

Mark 11:25–26

God Rejoices When a Man . . .

Anticipates Christ's Return

Behold what manner of love the Father has bestowed on us, that we should be called children of God! Therefore the world does not know us, because it did not know Him. Beloved, now we are children of God; and it has not yet been revealed what we shall be, but we know that when He is revealed, we shall be like Him, for we shall see Him as He is. And everyone who has this hope in Him purifies himself, just as He is pure.

1 John 3:1–3

Let not your heart be troubled; you believe in God, believe also in Me. In My Father's house are many mansions; if it were not so, I would have told you. I go to prepare a place for you. And if I go and prepare a place for you, I will come again and receive you to Myself; that where I am, there you may be also.

John 14:1–3

So the ransomed of the LORD shall return,
And come to Zion with singing,
With everlasting joy on their heads.
They shall obtain joy and gladness;
Sorrow and sighing shall flee away.

Isaiah 51:11

For behold, I create new heavens and a
    new earth;
And the former shall not be remembered
    or come to mind.
But be glad and rejoice forever in what I create;
For behold, I create Jerusalem as a rejoicing,
And her people a joy.
I will rejoice in Jerusalem,
And joy in My people;
The voice of weeping shall no longer
    be heard in her,
Nor the voice of crying.

Isaiah 65:17–19

For as the lightning comes from the east and flashes to the west, so also will the coming of the Son of Man be. For wherever the carcass is, there the eagles will be gathered together.

Immediately after the tribulation of those days the sun will be darkened, and the moon will not give its light; the stars will fall from heaven, and the powers of the heavens will be shaken. Then the sign of the Son of Man will appear in heaven, and then all the tribes of the earth will mourn, and they will see the Son of Man coming on the clouds of heaven with power and great glory. And He will send His angels with a great sound of a trumpet, and they will gather together His elect from the four winds, from one end of heaven to the other.

Matthew 24:27–31

There will be signs in the sun, in the moon, and in the stars; and on the earth distress of nations, with perplexity, the sea and the waves roaring; men's hearts failing them from fear and the expectation of those things which are coming on the earth, for the powers of the heavens will be shaken. Then they will see the Son of Man coming in a cloud with power and great glory. Now when these things begin to happen, look up and lift up your heads, because your redemption draws near.

Luke 21:25–28

The day of the Lord will come as a thief in the night, in which the heavens will pass away with a great noise, and the elements will melt with fervent heat; both the earth and the works that are in it will be burned up. Therefore, since all these things will be dissolved, what manner of persons ought you to be in holy conduct and godliness, looking for and hastening the coming of the day of God, because of which the heavens will be dissolved, being on fire, and the elements will melt with fervent heat?

2 Peter 3:10–12

Men of Galilee, why do you stand gazing up into heaven? This same Jesus, who was taken up from you into heaven, will so come in like manner as you saw Him go into heaven.

Acts 1:11

He who believes in the Son of God has the witness in himself; he who does not believe God has made Him a liar, because he has not believed the testimony that God has given of His Son. And this is the testimony: that God has given us eternal life, and this life is in His Son. He who has the Son has life; he who does not have the Son of God does not have life. These things I have written to you who believe in the name of the Son of God, that you may know that you have eternal life, and that you may continue to believe in the name of the Son of God.

1 John 5:10–13

And God will wipe away every tear from their eyes; there shall be no more death, nor sorrow, nor crying. There shall be no more pain, for the former things have passed away.

Revelation 21:4

Looking for the blessed hope and glorious appearing of our great God and Savior Jesus Christ.

Titus 2:13

Dedicates His Life to God

Their descendants shall be known among
      the Gentiles,
And their offspring among the people.
All who see them shall acknowledge them,
That they are the posterity whom the
      LORD has blessed.
I will greatly rejoice in the LORD,
My soul shall be joyful in my God;
For He has clothed me with the garments
      of salvation,
He has covered me with the robe of
      righteousness,
As a bridegroom decks himself with
      ornaments,
And as a bride adorns herself with her jewels.
For as the earth brings forth its bud,
As the garden causes the things that are
      sown in it to spring forth,
So the Lord GOD will cause righteousness
      and praise to spring forth before all the
      nations.

Isaiah 61:9–11

For I will pour water on him who is thirsty,
And floods on the dry ground;
I will pour My Spirit on your descendants,
And My blessing on your offspring.

Isaiah 44:3

For as many of you as were baptized into Christ have put on Christ. There is neither Jew nor Greek, there is neither slave nor free, there is neither male nor female; for you are all one in Christ Jesus. And if you are Christ's, then you are Abraham's seed, and heirs according to the promise.

Galatians 3:27–29

I am the vine, you are the branches. He who abides in Me, and I in him, bears much fruit; for without Me you can do nothing. If anyone does not abide in Me, he is cast out as a branch and is withered; and they gather them and throw them into the fire, and they are burned. If you abide in Me, and My words abide in you, you will ask what you desire, and it shall be done for you. By this My Father is glorified, that you bear much fruit; so you will be My disciples.

John 15:5–8

Most assuredly, I say to you, he who believes in Me, the works that I do he will do also; and greater works than these he will do, because I go to My Father. And whatever you ask in My name, that I will do, that the Father may be glorified in the Son. If you ask anything in My name, I will do it.

John 14:12–14

You did not choose Me, but I chose you and appointed you that you should go and bear fruit, and that your fruit should remain, that whatever you ask the Father in My name He may give you. These things I command you, that you love one another.

John 15:16–17

In that day you will ask Me nothing. Most assuredly, I say to you, whatever you ask the Father in My name He will give you. Until now you have asked nothing in My name. Ask, and you will receive, that your joy may be full.

John 16:23–24

Trusts and Waits for God's Answers 🍃

My soul, wait silently for God alone,
For my expectation is from Him.
He only is my rock and my salvation;
He is my defense;
I shall not be moved.
In God is my salvation and my glory;
The rock of my strength,
And my refuge, is in God.
Trust in Him at all times, you people;
Pour out your heart before Him;
God is a refuge for us.

Psalm 62:5–8

Let all those who hate Zion
Be put to shame and turned back.
Let them be as the grass on the housetops,
Which withers before it grows up,
With which the reaper does not fill his hand,
Nor he who binds sheaves, his arms.
Neither let those who pass by them say,
"The blessing of the LORD be upon you;
We bless you in the name of the LORD!"

Psalm 129:5–8

Every word of God is pure;
He is a shield to those who put their trust in
    Him.

Proverbs 30:5

I am the LORD, and there is no other;
There is no God besides Me.
I will gird you, though you have not known
    Me,
That they may know from the rising of the
    sun to its setting
That there is none besides Me.
I am the LORD, and there is no other.

Isaiah 45:5–6

The LORD your God in your midst,
The Mighty One, will save;
He will rejoice over you with gladness,
He will quiet you with His love,
He will rejoice over you with singing.

Zephaniah 3:17

Do not be deceived, my beloved brethren.
Every good gift and every perfect gift is from above,
and comes down from the Father of lights, with
whom there is no variation or shadow of turning.

James 1:16–17

For assuredly, I say to you, till heaven and earth pass away, one jot or one tittle will by no means pass from the law till all is fulfilled. Whoever therefore breaks one of the least of these commandments, and teaches men so, shall be called least in the kingdom of heaven; but whoever does and teaches them, he shall be called great in the kingdom of heaven. For I say to you, that unless your righteousness exceeds the righteousness of the scribes and Pharisees, you will by no means enter the kingdom of heaven.

Matthew 5:18–20

I waited patiently for the LORD;
And He inclined to me,
And heard my cry.

Psalm 40:1

Is Reconciled with His Brother

For He Himself is our peace, who has made both one, and has broken down the middle wall of separation, having abolished in His flesh the enmity, that is, the law of commandments contained in ordinances, so as to create in Himself one new man from the two, thus making peace, and that He might reconcile them both to God in one body through the cross, thereby putting to death the enmity. And He came and preached peace to you who were afar off and to those who were near. For through Him we both have access by one Spirit to the Father.

Ephesians 2:14–18

Moreover if your brother sins against you, go and tell him his fault between you and him alone. If he hears you, you have gained your brother.

Matthew 18:15

Where there is neither Greek nor Jew, circumcised nor uncircumcised, barbarian, Scythian, slave nor free, but Christ is all and in all.

Colossians 3:11

If someone says, "I love God," and hates his brother, he is a liar; for he who does not love his brother whom he has seen, how can he love God whom he has not seen?

1 John 4:20

Jesus said to him, "You shall love the LORD your God with all your heart, with all your soul, and with all your mind. This is the first and great commandment. And the second is like it: You shall love your neighbor as yourself. On these two commandments hang all the Law and the Prophets."

Matthew 22:37–40

Behold, how good and how pleasant it is
For brethren to dwell together in unity!

Psalm 133:1

The glory which You gave Me I have given them, that they may be one just as We are one: "I in them, and You in Me; that they may be made perfect in one, and that the world may know that You have sent Me, and have loved them as You have loved Me."

John 17:22–23

Dynamic Examples of
Godly Men . . .

Abraham

> Now the LORD had said to Abram:
> "Get out of your country,
> From your family
> And from your father's house,
> To a land that I will show you.
> I will make you a great nation;
> I will bless you
> And make your name great;
> And you shall be a blessing.
> I will bless those who bless you,
> And I will curse him who curses you;
> And in you all the families of the earth shall
> be blessed."
>
> *Genesis 12:1–3*

The LORD said to Abram, after Lot had separated from him: "Lift your eyes now and look from the place where you are—northward, southward, eastward, and westward; for all the land which you see I give to you and your descendants forever. And I will make your descendants as the dust of the earth; so that if a man could number the dust of the earth, then your descendants also could be numbered."

Genesis 13:14–16

After these things the word of the LORD came to Abram in a vision, saying, "Do not be afraid, Abram. I am your shield, your exceedingly great reward."

But Abram said, "Lord GOD, what will You give me, seeing I go childless, and the heir of my house is Eliezer of Damascus?" Then Abram said, "Look, You have given me no offspring; indeed one born in my house is my heir!"

And behold, the word of the LORD came to him, saying, "This one shall not be your heir, but one who will come from your own body shall be your heir." Then He brought him outside and said, "Look now toward heaven, and count the stars if you are able to number them." And He said to him, "So shall your descendants be."

And he believed in the LORD, and He accounted it to him for righteousness.

Genesis 15:1–6

Know that only those who are of faith are sons of Abraham. And the Scripture, foreseeing that God would justify the Gentiles by faith, preached the gospel to Abraham beforehand, saying, "In you all the nations shall be blessed." So then those who are of faith are blessed with believing Abraham.

Galatians 3:7–9

When Abram was ninety-nine years old, the LORD appeared to Abram and said to him, "I am Almighty God; walk before Me and be blameless. And I will make My covenant between Me and you, and will multiply you exceedingly." Then Abram fell on his face, and God talked with him, saying: "As for Me, behold, My covenant is with you, and you shall be a father of many nations. No longer shall your name be called Abram, but your name shall be Abraham; for I have made you a father of many nations."

Genesis 17:1–5

He opened the rock, and water gushed out;
It ran in the dry places like a river.
For He remembered His holy promise,
And Abraham His servant.
He brought out His people with joy,
His chosen ones with gladness.
He gave them the lands of the Gentiles,
And they inherited the labor of the nations,
That they might observe His statutes
And keep His laws.

Psalm 105:41–45

The LORD visited Sarah as He had said, and the LORD did for Sarah as He had spoken. For Sarah conceived and bore Abraham a son in his old age, at the set time of which God had spoken to him. And Abraham called the name of his son who was born to him—whom Sarah bore to him—Isaac. Then Abraham circumcised his son Isaac when he was eight days old, as God had commanded him. Now Abraham was one hundred years old when his son Isaac was born to him. And Sarah said, "God has made me laugh, and all who hear will laugh with me." She also said, "Who would have said to Abraham that Sarah would nurse children? For I have borne him a son in his old age."

So the child grew and was weaned. And Abraham made a great feast on the same day that Isaac was weaned.

Genesis 21:1–8

Jacob 🍃

Sing aloud to God our strength;
Make a joyful shout to the God of Jacob
Raise a song and strike the timbrel,
The pleasant harp with the lute.
Blow the trumpet at the time of the New
     Moon,
At the full moon, on our solemn feast day.
For this is a statute for Israel,
A law of the God of Jacob.
I am the LORD your God,
Who brought you out of the land of Egypt;
Open your mouth wide, and I will fill it.

Psalm 81:1–4, 10

Then God said to Jacob, "Arise, go up to Bethel and dwell there; and make an altar there to God, who appeared to you when you fled from the face of Esau your brother."

And Jacob said to his household and to all who were with him, "Put away the foreign gods that are among you, purify yourselves, and change your garments. Then let us arise and go up to Bethel; and I will make an altar there to God, who answered me in the day of my distress and has been with me in the way which I have gone."

Genesis 35:1–3

Then Jacob was left alone; and a Man wrestled with him until the breaking of day. Now when He saw that He did not prevail against him, He touched the socket of his hip; and the socket of Jacob's hip was out of joint as He wrestled with him. And He said, "Let Me go, for the day breaks."

But he said, "I will not let You go unless You bless me!"

So He said to him, "What is your name?"

He said, "Jacob."

And He said, "Your name shall no longer be called Jacob, but Israel; for you have struggled with God and with men, and have prevailed."

Then Jacob asked, saying, "Tell me Your name, I pray."

And He said, "Why is it that you ask about My name?"

And He blessed him there. And Jacob called the name of the place Peniel: "For I have seen God face to face, and my life is preserved."

Genesis 32:24–30

Then they sent the tunic of many colors, and they brought it to their father and said, "We have found this. Do you know whether it is your son's tunic or not?"

And he recognized it and said, "It is my son's tunic. A wild beast has devoured him. Without doubt Joseph is torn to pieces." Then Jacob tore his clothes, put sackcloth on his waist, and mourned for his son many days. And all his sons and all his daughters arose to comfort him; but he refused to be comforted, and he said, "For I shall go down into the grave to my son in mourning." Thus his father wept for him.

Genesis 37:32–35

Joseph 🍃

To Joseph were born two sons before the years of famine came, whom Asenath, the daughter of Poti-Pherah priest of On, bore to him. Joseph called the name of the firstborn Manasseh: "For God has made me forget all my toil and all my father's house." And the name of the second he called Ephraim: "For God has caused me to be fruitful in the land of my affliction."

Then the seven years of plenty which were in the land of Egypt ended, and the seven years of famine began to come, as Joseph had said. The famine was in all lands, but in all the land of Egypt there was bread. So when all the land of Egypt was famished, the people cried to Pharaoh for bread. Then Pharaoh said to all the Egyptians, "Go to Joseph; whatever he says to you, do." The famine was over all the face of the earth, and Joseph opened all the storehouses and sold to the Egyptians. And the famine became severe in the land of Egypt. So all countries came to Joseph in Egypt to buy grain, because the famine was severe in all lands.

Genesis 41:50–57

Then Joseph could not restrain himself before all those who stood by him, and he cried out, "Make everyone go out from me!" So no one stood with him while Joseph made himself known to his brothers. And he wept aloud, and the Egyptians and the house of Pharaoh heard it. Then Joseph said to his brothers, "I am Joseph; does my father still live?" But his brothers could not answer him, for they were dismayed in his presence. And Joseph said to his brothers, "Please come near to me." So they came near. Then he said: "I am Joseph your brother, whom you sold into Egypt. But now, do not therefore be grieved or angry with yourselves because you sold me here; for God sent me before you to preserve life. For these two years the famine has been in the land, and there are still five years in which there will be neither plowing nor harvesting. And God sent me before you to preserve a posterity for you in the earth, and to save your lives by a great deliverance. So now it was not you who sent me here, but God; and He has made me a father to Pharaoh, and lord of all his house, and a ruler throughout all the land of Egypt.

"Hurry and go up to my father, and say to him, 'Thus says your son Joseph: "God has made me lord of all Egypt; come down to me, do not tarry. You shall dwell in the land of Goshen, and you shall be near to me, you and your children, your children's children, your flocks and your herds, and all that you have."

Genesis 45:1–10

Then Joseph fell on his father's face, and wept over him, and kissed him.

Genesis 50:1

Then Joseph provided his father, his brothers, and all his father's household with bread, according to the number in their families.

Genesis 47:12

Then Israel saw Joseph's sons, and said, "Who are these?"

Joseph said to his father, "They are my sons, whom God has given me in this place."

And he said, "Please bring them to me, and I will bless them." Now the eyes of Israel were dim with age, so that he could not see. Then Joseph brought them near him, and he kissed them and embraced them.

Genesis 48:8–10

David

> Arise, O LORD, to Your resting place,
> You and the ark of Your strength.
> Let Your priests be clothed with righteousness,
> And let Your saints shout for joy.
> For Your servant David's sake,
> Do not turn away the face of Your Anointed.
> The LORD has sworn in truth to David;
> He will not turn from it:
> I will set upon your throne the fruit of
>   your body.
> If your sons will keep My covenant
> And My testimony which I shall teach them,
> Their sons also shall sit upon your throne
>   forevermore.
> For the LORD has chosen Zion;
> He has desired it for His dwelling place:
> This is My resting place forever;
> Here I will dwell, for I have desired it.
> I will abundantly bless her provision;
> I will satisfy her poor with bread.
> I will also clothe her priests with salvation,
> And her saints shall shout aloud for joy.
> There I will make the horn of David grow;
> I will prepare a lamp for My Anointed.
> His enemies I will clothe with shame,
> But upon Himself His crown shall flourish.
>
> *Psalm 132:8–18*

Incline your ear, and come to Me.
Hear, and your soul shall live;
And I will make an everlasting covenant
    with you—
The sure mercies of David.
Indeed I have given him as a witness to
    the people,
A leader and commander for the people.

Isaiah 55:3–4

David said to his son Solomon, "Be strong and of good courage, and do it; do not fear nor be dismayed, for the LORD God—my God—will be with you. He will not leave you nor forsake you, until you have finished all the work for the service of the house of the LORD."

1 Chronicles 28:20

As for you, if you walk before Me as your father David walked, and do according to all that I have commanded you, and if you keep My statutes and My judgments, then I will establish the throne of your kingdom, as I covenanted with David your father, saying, "You shall not fail to have a man as ruler in Israel."

2 Chronicles 7:17–18

Then David spoke to the LORD the words of this song, on the day when the LORD had delivered him from the hand of all his enemies, and from the hand of Saul.

"For You are my lamp, O LORD;
The LORD shall enlighten my darkness.
For by You I can run against a troop;
By my God I can leap over a wall.
As for God, His way is perfect;
The word of the LORD is proven;
He is a shield to all who trust in Him.
For who is God, except the LORD?
And who is a rock, except our God?
God is my strength and power,
And He makes my way perfect.
He makes my feet like the feet of deer,
And sets me on my high places.
He teaches my hands to make war,
So that my arms can bend a bow of bronze.
You have also given me the shield of Your
    salvation;
Your gentleness has made me great."

2 Samuel 22:1, 29-36

Noah

So the LORD said, "I will destroy man whom I have created from the face of the earth, both man and beast, creeping thing and birds of the air, for I am sorry that I have made them." But Noah found grace in the eyes of the LORD.

This is the genealogy of Noah. Noah was a just man, perfect in his generations. Noah walked with God. And Noah begot three sons: Shem, Ham, and Japheth.

Genesis 6:7–10

Then the LORD said to Noah, "Come into the ark, you and all your household, because I have seen that you are righteous before Me in this generation."

So Noah, with his sons, his wife, and his sons' wives, went into the ark because of the waters of the flood.

Genesis 7:1, 7

So God blessed Noah and his sons, and said to them: "Be fruitful and multiply, and fill the earth."

Then God spoke to Noah and to his sons with him, saying: "And as for Me, behold, I establish My covenant with you and with your descendants after you."

Genesis 9:1, 8–9

So He destroyed all living things which were on the face of the ground: both man and cattle, creeping thing and bird of the air. They were destroyed from the earth. Only Noah and those who were with him in the ark remained alive. And the waters prevailed on the earth one hundred and fifty days.

Then God remembered Noah, and every living thing, and all the animals that were with him in the ark. And God made a wind to pass over the earth, and the waters subsided.

Genesis 7:23–8:1

Without faith it is impossible to please Him, for he who comes to God must believe that He is, and that He is a rewarder of those who diligently seek Him.

By faith Noah, being divinely warned of things not yet seen, moved with godly fear, prepared an ark for the saving of his household, by which he condemned the world and became heir of the righteousness which is according to faith.

Hebrews 11:6–7

Paul

As he journeyed he came near Damascus, and suddenly a light shone around him from heaven. Then he fell to the ground, and heard a voice saying to him, "Saul, Saul, why are you persecuting Me?"

And he said, "Who are You, Lord?"

Then the Lord said, "I am Jesus, whom you are persecuting. It is hard for you to kick against the goads."

So he, trembling and astonished, said, "Lord, what do You want me to do?"

Then the Lord said to him, "Arise and go into the city, and you will be told what you must do."

And the men who journeyed with him stood speechless, hearing a voice but seeing no one. Then Saul arose from the ground, and when his eyes were opened he saw no one. But they led him by the hand and brought him into Damascus. And he was three days without sight, and neither ate nor drank.

Acts 9:3–9

At midnight Paul and Silas were praying and singing hymns to God, and the prisoners were listening to them. Suddenly there was a great earthquake, so that the foundations of the prison were shaken; and immediately all the doors were opened and everyone's chains were loosed. And the keeper of the prison, awaking from sleep and seeing the prison doors open, supposing the prisoners had fled, drew his sword and was about to kill himself. But Paul called with a loud voice, saying, "Do yourself no harm, for we are all here."

Then he called for a light, ran in, and fell down trembling before Paul and Silas. And he brought them out and said, "Sirs, what must I do to be saved?"

So they said, "Believe on the LORD Jesus Christ, and you will be saved, you and your household." Then they spoke the word of the LORD to him and to all who were in his house. And he took them the same hour of the night and washed their stripes. And immediately he and all his family were baptized. Now when he had brought them into his house, he set food before them; and he rejoiced, having believed in God with all his household.

Acts 16:25–34

For I consider that the sufferings of this present time are not worthy to be compared with the glory which shall be revealed in us. For the earnest expectation of the creation eagerly waits for the revealing of the sons of God. For the creation was subjected to futility, not willingly, but because of Him who subjected it in hope; because the creation itself also will be delivered from the bondage of corruption into the glorious liberty of the children of God. For we know that the whole creation groans and labors with birth pangs together until now. Not only that, but we also who have the firstfruits of the Spirit, even we ourselves groan within ourselves, eagerly waiting for the adoption, the redemption of our body. For we were saved in this hope, but hope that is seen is not hope; for why does one still hope for what he sees? But if we hope for what we do not see, we eagerly wait for it with perseverance.

Likewise the Spirit also helps in our weaknesses. For we do not know what we should pray for as we ought, but the Spirit Himself makes intercession for us with groanings which cannot be uttered. Now He who searches the hearts knows what the mind of the Spirit is, because He makes intercession for the saints according to the will of God.

Romans 8:18–27

Lest I should be exalted above measure by the abundance of the revelations, a thorn in the flesh was given to me, a messenger of Satan to buffet me, lest I be exalted above measure. Concerning this thing I pleaded with the Lord three times that it might depart from me. And He said to me, "My grace is sufficient for you, for My strength is made perfect in weakness." Therefore most gladly I will rather boast in my infirmities, that the power of Christ may rest upon me. Therefore I take pleasure in infirmities, in reproaches, in needs, in persecutions, in distresses, for Christ's sake. For when I am weak, then I am strong.

2 Corinthians 12:7–10

Now the Lord spoke to Paul in the night by a vision, "Do not be afraid, but speak, and do not keep silent; for I am with you, and no one will attack you to hurt you; for I have many people in this city." And he continued there a year and six months, teaching the word of God among them.

Acts 18:9–11

Are they Hebrews? So am I. Are they Israelites? So am I. Are they the seed of Abraham? So am I. Are they ministers of Christ?—I speak as a fool—I am more: in labors more abundant, in stripes above measure, in prisons more frequently, in deaths often. From the Jews five times I received forty stripes minus one. Three times I was beaten with rods; once I was stoned; three times I was shipwrecked; a night and a day I have been in the deep; in journeys often, in perils of waters, in perils of robbers, in perils of my own countrymen, in perils of the Gentiles, in perils in the city, in perils in the wilderness, in perils in the sea, in perils among false brethren; in weariness and toil, in sleeplessness often, in hunger and thirst, in fastings often, in cold and nakedness—besides the other things, what comes upon me daily: my deep concern for all the churches. Who is weak, and I am not weak? Who is made to stumble, and I do not burn with indignation?

If I must boast, I will boast in the things which concern my infirmity. The God and Father of our Lord Jesus Christ, who is blessed forever, knows that I am not lying.

2 Corinthians 11:22–31

PRAYER REQUESTS . . .

_____

_____

_____

_____

_____

_____

_____

_____

_____

_____

_____

_____

_____

_____

_____

_____

_____

_____

_____

_____

_____

ANSWERED PRAYERS . . .

_____

_____

_____

_____

_____

_____

_____

_____

_____

_____

_____

_____

_____

_____

_____

_____

_____

_____

_____

_____

_____

_____

_____